THE CHRIST

THE CHRIST

*A Study of the God-Man Relationship
In the Whole of Creation and in
Jesus Christ*

PIET SCHOONENBERG, S.J.

HERDER AND HERDER

1971
HERDER AND HERDER NEW YORK
232 Madison Avenue, New York 10016

Original edition: *Hij is een God van Mensen,*
L. C. G. Malmberg N.V., 's-Hertogenbosch, 1969.
Translated by Della Couling.

Nihil obstat: Leo J. Steady
Imprimatur: + Robert F. Joyce
Burlington, November 24, 1970

Contents

Introduction

THIS book contains two theological studies, written for different purposes. The first one is an elaboration of a lecture given at the Catholic University of Nijmegen, The Netherlands. In this lecture, "God or Man: A False Dilemma," I inaugurated my career as ordinary professor of dogmatic theology at the same university. The text has been worked over several times since. In the years of my professorate christology has increasingly become my special field. Consequently, I became involved in the discussions on that type of christology which for us Catholics was normal and classical and seemed unchangeable. The questions, however, posed by the confrontation of this christology and modern ways of thinking, and by the proper history of this christology as well, forced me to critical reflection. The result is the second study in this book, "God and Man or God in Man?" Putting these two studies together, I added a "Conclusion" in which the basic insight present in both is confronted with God-is-dead theology. This does not mean that the latter is the most significant theological phenomenon of the past decade—happily it has turned out not to be. But God-is-dead theology was, however, a most serious challenge to theological thought.

The two studies presented in this book are both written from the same viewpoint—a believing viewpoint. God does not compete, God does not alienate. He does not dehumanize us, but makes us fully human, ultimately through his Word become man. As I have written elsewhere: our divinization is our humanization. Now I can add to that: Jesus' divine sonship is his human-ness to the utmost. I wanted to express this idea in the general title of this book. For the Dutch edition I chose a sentence which corresponds to scripture where it speaks of the God *of* Abraham, Isaac, and Jacob, the God *of* Israel and *of* Jesus Christ, the God who "is not ashamed to be called *their*

7

God" (Hebrews, 11, 16). The title of the book corresponded more exactly to a line of the eucharistic canon in *Your Word is Near* by Huub Oosterhuis (New York, 1968). The first reason for thanking God is formulated in this book as follows: "For you are a God of men" (p. 114). Hence the Dutch title of my book, *Hij is een God van Mensen* (He is a God of Men).

There are several reasons, however, for changing the title for the English edition, the most important being that this book may be confused with other ones which have nearly the same title. The new title, *The Christ*, points to the second study. But it may be used for the whole book, because most of all in the Christ God revealed himself as the God of men, and became our God. In the first study I tried to show that not only in creation in general but also in the gift of grace God is not competing but fulfilling. According to the second study the same holds true with regard to the person of Jesus Christ and his life, both in his earthly and in his glorified existence. In accordance with the terminology of Anglo-Saxon process thinking Christ can be called the "chief exemplification" of the God-man relationship, provided that he is also the source of God's fulfilling presence with mankind.

In both parts of this book I proceed tentatively. Since the Christian tradition is a history of continually ongoing interpretations and reinterpretations, no theology can be definitive. The theological renewal of our days is not definitive and my theology even less. I have suggested already that I evolved in my theological thinking. Some readers will notice that my viewpoints have developed more explicitly in the direction heralded in my book *Covenant and Creation* (London, Sheed and Ward, 1968), and that I have left behind me some of the ideas expressed in an earlier book on christology, published only in Dutch (*Het geloof van ons doopsel III*, 's Hertogenbosch, Malmberg, 1960). At this moment I welcome all criticism of my work, either by theologians or by the faithful community.

I am fully aware that there are fellow believers who are disturbed by the development of my thoughts. Others will say that I am not going far enough and am only fighting a rearguard action. For my part, I have no desire to be annexed either by progressives or by conservatives. In the crisis within Christian and particularly within Catholic thought I may perhaps contribute something by going my own way. This own way, which is, moreover, shared with others, is one of upholding and developing tradition, by opening the past to the present for the future. Past tradition itself is not a block but a movement: and it was mainly the study of christological discussions that made this point clear to me. This movement goes on in the present: now and in the future it can reach its most profound aims by finding the corrections it could not make fully before, by coming to the insights for which it was searching. Seen in this way the past is not a museum piece to be anxiously defended by conservatives and merely tolerated by progressives for the sake of pluriformity. The past is now "history," not in the sense, however, which this word usually has: not important for the present, but in the sense that the word ought to have: contributing to the ongoing of history in the present towards the future. In presenting the past in this way and by carrying on its movement I hope to contribute to the theology of today and tomorrow.

It was a pleasure for me to review the translation of this book during my recent stay in the United States. A result of this coincidence may be seen in the fact that I have added several notes referring to English and American theological writings. It was an experience for me to perceive to what extent ways of thinking on both sides of the ocean are parallel and how much we are all involved in one, though diversified, movement.

My heartfelt thanks to all those who have made this book possible: to those who have shared ideas, to the translator, to those who helped me in checking the translation, and to those who introduced me to the Anglo-Saxon theological world. For them all and for my readers I pray for the enlightenment of God's Spirit in this time of searching faith.

P. SCHOONENBERG, S.J.

THE CHRIST

I.

God or Man: A False Dilemma

THE present conflict between the theology of salvation history and existential theology would appear to rest on the assumption that metaphysical theology has become out of date. But that is still open to question. It depends on what one understands by metaphysics. If one means the projection of an ideal world behind or above the one in which we live—a sort of rationalized mythology—then metaphysics is indeed an unreal discussion, having not even the revealing character of myth. If one means the rationalizing of mystery, then it is even less serviceable for theology. Metaphysics can, however, also be the expression of the mystery that our real world does not conceal behind it, but is itself. Understood thus, in my opinion, metaphysical theology is not out of date. Then it is an unravellment of the question of God and world. It is in this sense that I have attempted here an exercise in metaphysical theology. I shall begin by recalling an earlier dispute in which metaphysical theology fell somewhat short of the mark, and then attempt in the light of modern thought to find the way to a better solution.

GOD OR MAN:
A DILEMMA OF YESTERDAY AND TODAY

After having separated in the sixteenth century, the Reformation and the Catholic Church show in the seventeenth century, at least to those looking back on their history, their common bond: they are struggling with the same Christian problem. This problem is that of reconciling God's merciful and sovereign rule on the one hand with the freedom and responsibility of man on the other. In the Calvinism within the Seven United Netherlands where, during a truce in the war against Spain, "Gommer and Armijn at Court/Haggle over the true faith," predestination was the main bone of contention. In Spain itself, by the end of the sixteenth century, the conflict was already in full flood between Molina and Báñez, but by the turn of the century the dispute had shifted its ground to Rome Now too predestination still figured in an important role, but the central issue had become the relation between the influence of God's actual grace and human freedom. Broadly speaking, we can thus say that within Calvinism the relation of God's predestination to salvation history, especially to the fall, thus its supralapsarian or infralapsarian character, came to the fore, while within Catholicism it was rather the implicit controversy therein over God's causality and man's freedom.

The Catholic dispute on grace entered history as one between two religious orders, the Dominican and the Jesuit. At first sight we can characterize the contraposition by naming the Dominicans of that time "theists" and the Jesuits "humanists," although it is perhaps open to question whether their spiritual descendants would agree to these labels. The Jesuit theologians more or less allied themselves with Luis de Molina, for whom the point of departure was the free will of the man responsible before God. For Molina no causal influence of God on human freedom itself is possible: he acts only together with our freedom.[1] For that reason there is no grace efficacious in itself, God guides our decisions to salvation through adapting the gift of his grace to the knowledge he has of human actions. For God knows what man in given real circumstances will do and he also knows—here is where the famous *scientia media* comes in—what man in other non-real circumstances *would* do.[2] In a correspondence with the Dominican theologian Garrigou-Lagrange someone wrote of the Molinists: "They always confront us with the curious image of a God in need of the spectacles of the *scientia*

1. Ludovicus Molina, *Concordia liberi arbitrii cum gratiae donis divina praescientia providentia praedestinatione et reprobatione*, Paris, Lethielleux, 1876. In q. 14, art. 13, disp. 26, 29, and 37.
2. *Ibid.*, disp. 52 and 53.

media in order to discover what man will do and of a great deal of diplomacy in order to adapt his rule accordingly."[3]

Domingo Báñez, Molina's chief opponent, forcefully posited God's total causality, which also moves the free will to decision from within, the *praedeterminatio physica,* and therefore the efficacy of grace from itself and no thanks to human acquiescence. He and his supporters present a very majestic image of God and impress one with the coherence of their system. It has, however, been doubted whether in this system human freedom is maintained more than with words alone. The answer seems to depend on another question: whether here God's influence places a new reality between faculty and its operation, comparable to the influence which is added to an instrument.[4] Here similarly the question arises of whether God is here transcendent-creative or categorical-intervening cause. The Dominican Sertillanges once wrote, as a clear criticism of Báñezianism, that God's causality with regard to the act of free will is not *prae,* not a *determinatio,* and not *physica,* seeing that it is creation.[5] And not long ago Karl Rahner criticized the *concursus* doctrine of the Molinists together with the Báñezian concept of God's causality.[6]

That Rahner criticizes both systems just in passing in a book devoted to other problems seems to be symptomatic. The conflict on grace and the metaphysical dispute inherent within it are no

---

3. "*On ne persistera pas moins . . . à nous présenter la singulière image de Dieu, qui a besoin des lunettes de la science moyenne pour découvrir les futurs contingents et de beaucoup de diplomatie pour y ajuster son gouvernement.*" R. Garrigou-Lagrange, *Dieu, Son Existence et sa Nature,* 2nd ed., Paris, 1950, p. 841. The writer adds here that this correspondent is not a Dominican.

4. For example, for a follower such as Joseph Gredt, *Elementa philosophiae aristotelico-thomisticae,* II ed 2a., Freiburg, 1912, p. 231.

5. A. Sertillanges, *Saint Thomas d'Aquin* I, 2nd ed., Paris, 1912, p. 265: ". . . *on commet . . . une triple hérésie verbale. Hérésie quant au plan de l'action qui n'est pas le plan 'physique,' mais le plan ontologique; hérésie quant à sa forme, qui n'est pas proprement 'motion' mais création; hérésie quant à sa mesure, qui n'est pas temporelle (prae) mais immobile et adéquate à l'éternité.*" See criticism of this point by Garrigou-Lagrange, *op. cit.,* p. 482, footnote. In *L'idée de création et ses retentissements en philosophie,* Paris, 1945, p. 187, Sertillanges vindicates his position but speaks of "*équivoque verbale.*"

6. Karl Rahner, "Hominisation as a theological Problem" in *Hominisation,* New York, 1968.

longer central issues because over the years the weaknesses of both positions have become apparent. Already in 1607, when Pope Paul V—more restrained in this dispute than the synod of Dordrecht in the Calvinist one—considered the question unripe for decision.[7] After that the conflict occasionally flickered into life again, as for example at the beginning of the twentieth century and more recently after the First World War. But it can no longer summon the old urgency. Since the Second World War it has been not the spiritualities of orders but the differences in generation which have formed the foundation of theological disputes. Moreover, it is becoming ever more clear that the mistake of both parties lay not primarily in what each defended, nor even in attacks on one another, but much more in an implicit presupposition on which they were of one mind. This was that the truths which both adhered to needed to be reconciled. That means that Creator and created are rivals, that God's activity is at the cost of man, and that man's freedom and originality at the cost of God's causality, that God is less active where man is more so and vice versa. It would now seem as though this presupposition has more or less been overcome and that the dispute on grace, at least so far as its central question is concerned, thus belongs to history, or rather to those sections of the past which no longer help to construct our history.

But it is not so simple. The saying "history repeats itself" continues to have meaning, although taken literally it is precisely the denial of what is proper to history. The old dispute repeats itself, but in a completely new way. It is true that it has had its day if we limit it to the specific position it occupied within a specific thought structure. The precise question on the relation between the total causality of God and the freedom of man need no longer be raised within scholastic theology. But in its generality the dispute has not over. The earlier controversy is an exponent of a question alive in all theistic thought, a question which even penetrates into a great deal of atheism, and which is indeed born from a certain response to it.

Thus within theism Molina's outlook reappears in the Jewish

---

7. Denzinger, *Enchiridion Symbolorum*, n. 1090; ed. A. Schönmetzer, Barcinone, 1963, n. 1997. All subsequent quotations are taken from the Schönmetzer edition and indicated by DS and their number.

philosopher Emmanuel Levinas, who nevertheless is not dependent on Molina and thinks in completely different categories. For Levinas there must be human freedom to encounter God, which always occurs in one's fellow man. Although God is creative in this encounter with regard to our freedom, this creating may not be understood in any way as causality, it is rather the offering and revealing of oneself as the Other.[8] In theological terms we could say that for Levinas creation coincides with covenant. Presently we shall return this stimulating philosophy, but for the moment we mention it only to illustrate the fact that the problem of Molina is again being lived in a different world of thought. But the accent on human freedom also leads to atheism. For Sartre's Orestes, Jupiter cannot be God, because the existence of God is an attack on men, who for good or ill wish to be themselves.[9] This is the theme of Sartre's plays and philosophical works, as also of the works of Camus and Jeanson. "Theism" is becoming even the term for accepting a god who eliminates or threatens man and the world, so that Paul Tillich proposes to surmount theism and atheism equally. Indeed, according to Tillich, the word "God" itself is so tainted with such notions that he suggests not using it for a generation. Following upon him were those authors generally gathered under the rubric of "God is dead."

At first sight this is all rather alarming. On closer examination the alarming element lies mainly in the fact that things could come to such a pass in our Christian thinking on God, and especially in our Christian life. Today our affirmation of God is all too often shrivelled and falsified by a neglect of or contempt for creation, and in particular for man. Not only do our natural and human sciences indicate earthly causes where formerly we thought to see God alone at work, but also there is a positivist tendency, especially in Anglo-

8. Emmanuel Levinas, *Totalité et Infini. Essai sur l'extériorité,* The Hague, 1961. See J. Plat, "De mens en de oneindige Ander bij Emmanuel Levinas," in *Tijdschrift voor Filosofie* 26 (1964), 457–500.

9. Jean-Paul Sartre, *Les Mouches,* 19th ed., Paris, 1943, pp. 132ff.; see Fr. Jeanson, "Athéisme et liberté," *Lumière et Vie* 13 (1954), 85–96. Catholic theology has recently been confronted with the neo-Marxist philosopher Ernst Bloch, who opposes God and human freedom more in the line of final causality: if the plenitude of perfection which is God already exists, then history loses its tension towards completion and thus its meaning.

Saxon thought, that is making it ever more difficult to affirm together God and man, God and world. But this by no means proves that the affirmation of God is in a hopeless situation. Rather the case is the opposite. Criticism of the concept of God creates scope for a deeper affirmation of God, and it is indeed conceivable that this affirmation is actually announced in that criticism—that is, that God's Spirit is precisely at work in the criticism of God. We may be optimistic with Bishop John Robinson and we may furthermore think not only with Tillich, but also along the lines of a renewed Thomism, as led by such authors as Sertillanges and Karl Rahner.

What follows will, we hope, contribute a little more light on the conflict. As a contribution to theology it can be no more than theory, but we may perhaps aspire to offer something of what *theoria* means, namely, contemplation which gives life form. What we wish to say is based on the word of revelation living in scripture and the Church, for theology is illumination of existence based in this word, translation of this word in our ever-new human situation. Our personal thought has also trodden the path of the biblical affirmation of God to the modern problem. Here we have developed from the Báñezian image of God to the view that God's transcendent creative causality does not detract from the reality of man and world but precisely affirms it. This view has, moreover, become common property among present-day Catholic theologians, although it has not yet found a commonly accepted lucid formulation on all points: we are thinking here of the "immediate creation of the soul." The problems must really begin in the field most peculiar to theology, the examination of God's salvific acts of redemption and giving grace. Is here too, one might ask, the question of "God or man" a false dilemma? Do God and man always concur in God's gift of grace? Is this concurrence just as necessary here as in God's creative rule of the world? Or does precisely the supernatural character of this salvific act say that here God alone contracts a bond with man, independently of all mutual union between men? Does not God's completely unmerited sharing of self with his creation, which is still forgiveness and redemption for sinful man, relate "vertically" to all "horizontal" bonds within the created world itself? Does it not come, to use Barthian terms, "vertically from above"?

We wish to speak in particular of these questions concerning God's supernatural grace. But for the sake of clarity we think it

18

well to sum up first in a few points what we may affirm concerning the concurrence of God and creature in his creative running of the world. After that we shall discuss God's saving activity. This division is merely for practical reasons. We do not intend to suggest that God's act of salvation is extrinsically added to his creation. It is even possible that it is included in it, but this is a point that can be left to the end.

GOD AND WORLDLY CAUSE CONCUR

In the historical survey above the words "creation" and "causality" of God have been used without distinction. Personally we are quite willing, with reference to God, to exchange the term "causality" for a better one, if there is any. We use this term here because precisely within the category of "causality" we see the total transcendence of God and the total analogy between the Infinite and the finite. In this our thoughts are often stimulated or completed by those of Karl Rahner.[10] He can bring us to the view that God's causality does not stand on the same level with those of creatures, that God does not begin a work that we must take over and complete, that he does not complete what we do not achieve, that he does not replace created causes by intervention or intercession. It appears to be a mark of homage to the Creator if, on the origin of a new level of being, on the origin of a new person, on an unpredicted turn of history, he is supposed to realize from outside what the cosmos from inside does not achieve. On closer inspection, however, this is wronging God's honor by placing him on the same level with worldly causes, and the fact is being ignored that he is already active within them. If we affirm God completely as Creator, then it is he who makes the whole world be and act. He realizes all the finite not only through the whole essence of it, but also through continued existence and activity. The Creator makes all being and doing, in evolution, history, and salvation history. He realizes all being and activity in the world as a being and activity of the worldly beings themselves.

The concept of a God who himself acts among men and things is

---

10. Karl Rahner, *op. cit.*, n. 6; and in "Theos in the New Testament," in *Theological Investigations I,* Baltimore and Dublin, 1966; "Modern Christological Problems," in *ibid.*; "Christology Within an Evolutive World View," in *Theological Investigations V,* Baltimore and Dublin, 1966.

to be found in holy scripture, especially with the oldest narrator of the Old Testament the Yahwist, and there this concept is a symbol of God's mighty and tender care. But there is also to be found the tendency to pass beyond this concept and thus to safeguard God's super-worldly and universal rule. For the Elohist God does not intervene beside men, but leads men from within through dreams. The concept of the Yahwist is, moreover, modified by making the "angel of Yahweh" appear in place of Yahweh himself. The Apocalyptic writings see angels and devils as the executors of God's world rule. The book of Wisdom and the epistle to the Romans approach the view that within God's creation sin punishes itself. This tendency and the many confirmations of God's all-embracing creative works take us beyond the idea of a creative act which only occurs "in the beginning"—if this term is restricted in Scripture to asserting a chronological beginning—to the concept of a continuous creation. We understand then that Jesus says precisely on the Sabbath, the day of God's rest, "My Father is working still" (John 5, 17). For he is the "one God the Father from whom are all things" (I Corinthians 8, 6).

What the Bible says is confirmed by our reason. When God creates "from nothing" (2 Maccabees 7, 28), then this means on the one hand that nothing and no one other than God is the ultimate foundation of all the world, and on the other hand that nothing in this world has an ultimate foundation other than God, that *everything in all respects* finds its foundation in him—thus also in continued existence, development, and history, in the achieving of completion. God's care for continued existence is not distinct from his creating. Only in created reality itself can a distinction be made between beginning and continued existence, but the dependence on God's total causality is the same in both. Only for us, who never are the cause of anything in all its reality, is "all beginning difficult," while the result of our work subsequently more or less stands on its own. That the world is also able to stand on its own is also just as much a work and a gift of and on origination from God, and requires from him, so to speak, no more than the causation of further existence. This is equally true for the activity and self-development of all reality, even of us, for just as the Creator gives it to the created to be itself, so he gives it to act for itself and to develop for itself.

Thus it is quite clear that all activity in the world is borne by God's continuous creation. But is it not also true that God never works by intervention, in the stead of creatures, that on the contrary he realizes all through making his world realize itself? This question must also be answered in the affirmative. The argument in its favor can be presented in different ways. Philosophically the whole relationship between God and world—and thus that which in theology is called "creation"—can be described as participation. Each worldly being—any creature, theologically speaking—participates in its own way in God's being, but in the concrete being of God; not merely in a "metaphysical essence," in a fullness of being such as we conceive it, but in a God concretely creative, continuously realizing the world, and thus also in God's continuous creation. Each creature participates in its own way in God's act of creation with regard to all creatures (to all other creatures, but also to itself: in the manner of its own level of being the creature is *causa sui*). The creature thus always has, in its way, within its own limited possibilities, a part in the realizing of its fellow-creatures, and it is in this measure included by the Creator in his continuous creation.

A confirmation of this view is found in a consideration of the world's unity. This unity requires that all worldly beings also participate in one another, be with and in one another, and this finds its highest realization in our knowing and giving meaning. But by so doing they are also of one another, and realize one another. Certainly, new realities constantly arise. But they are not alien, at least not entirely alien, otherwise the old and the new would not belong to one and the same cosmos. The new comes not only from outside into the world, therefore, it must also in its way be from within the world—or in other words: the newly created is produced with the help of worldly causes.

The late Herman Fortmann once wrote that the expression "from outside," applied to God's creating and even to God's revelation, is not a very apt one: "God never acts in anything really from outside, because he is present in everything that exists distinct from him as the deepest foundation of that existence, as Creator. He is not encompassed by what exists distinct from him, but he is certainly always more deeply present in it than my deepest self in me." Nevertheless, said Fortmann, the possibility of an intervention of God may not be

21

denied, yet in such a way that "God intervenes from within his creation."[11] But what precisely do these words mean? If an intervention from within is something different from an intervention from outside, in what then does the difference lie? The answer is precisely in the fact that God, *as* immanent in his creatures, thus in his relationship with them, thus together with them, causes a certain reality to be realized. In other words, in the realization of something new he works through the already existing.

CREATION, EVOLUTION, HISTORY

It will be worth our while to elaborate this relation more fully in regard to creation, evolution, and history. Our summary does not intend, however, to indicate a sequence in time. For precisely now it seems that creation is not an event at the beginning of our history, but the relation which exists between the whole world in the whole of its history on the one hand and the infinite God on the other. "Creation" does not add anything to the relation between God and world—the word merely expresses the activity of this relation, it says that in this relation God is always the one who realizes the world in all its components and aspects and that on the other hand the world is completely and wholly realized by God, from God, and in God. Briefly expressed: the world receives its reality as its own from God. Just as creation is hardly a distinct event "in the beginning," so is it certainly not an event which later occurs from time to time. The world is a becoming world, a world ever surpassing itself, where the new proceeds from the old and yet, *at the same time,* is new and more. And precisely as such, as becoming and self-surpassing, the world is realized by God. Precisely as from the old and yet as more than the old, each new reality is realized by God—not by an addition from outside, not by additionally creating something. It is thus also useless to distinguish, as is so often done, between immediate and mediate creation. Everything in the world can be called mediately created insofar as it is at the same time derived from something else; but everything in the world must, just as the world

11. Herman Fortmann, "Enkele voorlopige notities bij een artikel over Maria's maagdelijkheid," *Theologie en zielzorg* 62 (1966), 283–291; quotations on pp. 287–289.

as a whole, also and above all be called immediately created, for God the creator is everywhere equally near and immanent. Here we should not let ourselves be misled by the expression "creation from nothing." It refers to the independence that the creating God has with regard to whatever is outside him, and thus to the dependence which the world *as a whole* has with regard to God alone. The expression "creation from nothing" may not, however, suggest that God first allows something to emerge from nothing and then introduces it into the existent world. From nothing, that is, independently of anything whatever, God constantly creates a world in which one thing proceeds from another.[12]

This concept expresses too what God's creation means in connection with evolution. Of foremost importance here are the various evolutionary stages wherein not only *varying* forms emerge, but truly *higher* ones as in, for example, the (hypothetical) development of living beings from non-living and that of man from animals. Here the difference between higher and lower is real as well as is the development of the higher from the lower. As for the dilemma either that man, because he has developed from an animal, is not essentially higher (materialism), or that he is essentially higher than the animal and thus cannot be developed from it (a form of spiritualism)—once we have accepted the difference between both grades of being and the development of higher from lower as real, then we can see it as the highest form of "self-surpassing" inherent in all being. Such a term, coined by Karl Rahner,[13] means that the reality

12. God's ongoing creation of a developing world demands a rethinking of his eternity. Robert E. Joyce in Chapter 8 of a book written by him and his wife (Mary Rosera Joyce and Robert E. Joyce, *New Dynamics in Sexual Love,* Collegeville, 1970, pp. 81–91: "Estrangement") conceives of God's creation as "an eternal act. We are given a being like our Creator's—an eternal being, but not eternal in an unlimited way" (p. 90). Hence, "Communications [which are opposed to 'communion'], time, space, and evolution are all consequences of our estrangement right within the paradise of creation and incarnation" (p. 91). More realistic is a chapter of Eulalio R. Baltazar's book, *God Within Process* (New York, 1970) entitled "Eternity as the Fullness of Time" (pp. 106–130). Here the positive value of time (or: of evolution in time) is emphasized and God's eternity is seen not as the absence but as the fullness of time itself. (Our criticism of Robert Joyce does not take away our high esteem for the Joyces' plea for true sexual freedom which is basic to their book.)

13. Rahner, *Hominisation* (note 6).

23

of the world in its origin both remains itself and surpasses itself. A product, a fruit, a child is always brought about in some way or other, but it is at the same time new and more with regard to its makers or parents. In man the child, from the moment of its origin, is at the same time the person who confronts his parents. These leaps are inherent in every being: they are already there in the development of the same being, they show themselves more clearly in the origin of a new being, they are greatest when a higher level is achieved. It is that the Creator realizes, everywhere, also and in particular in evolution. He does not add anything from outside, but realizes the leap which the world makes from inside.

In this light it is in fact superfluous to speak separately of the origin of man, of hominisation. But the consideration of such origin, and of every individual man, has been complicated for centuries by our distinction between soul and body. We are accustomed to the formula that the soul is created or infused immediately by God. Yet we call the parents father and mother of the child, and not only of his body. As I have already said, at the same time that the child comes into being he from the outset confronts his parents, and at a human level, that is, as person. In view of the fact that the spiritual soul is the principle of this personhood, it is also the principle by which the child as person confronts the parents, and following that view the soul is not from and out of the parents. We express this by saying that it is immediately created, but by virtue of what has just been said on creation this should not be exclusively understood. The expression "infusion of the soul" is strongly dualistic as concerns the human image and suggests a co-creating from outside; it is then better avoided.

Until now we have been describing an event in nature; even in human propagation we discussed only this aspect. This leads us to say a few further words about the *natural laws,* meaning here the biological, physical, chemical laws and not the natural law referred to in morals, which could rather be called the personal norm. Two things can be said in our consideration of the natural laws. First, that God does not impose them from above, but realizes them along with nature itself as the constant manner of behavior proper to that nature. And further: that God neither abolishes the natural laws from above nor thwarts them from within. Each natural law states that a certain factor causes a certain phenomenon; it must also leave open the possibility of other modifying factors in a given case. This happens, for example, in the miracle. Certainly, the miracle is much more than a physical or biological exception, it is first and foremost a sign from God in his salvific dialogue with man. But the miracle is also an exception, and precisely in this aspect God does not oppose a natural law, but his grace evokes modifying factors from within the world itself, so as, for example, to give man new powers through his faith. The miracle is a special work of God, not because he eliminates earthly forces, but precisely because he enlists as many of them as possible as signs of the eternal life that he will give in the new heaven and the new earth. For so far as the miracle is a fact (whether or not it is announced as fact as we understand it, it is finally a question for exegesis), it is a real sign and a portent of the completion, the "universal restoration" (Acts 3, 21), towards which creation is heading.[14]

Everything we have said or could still say about the relation between God's work of creation and nature can eventually be summed up as follows: God realizes nature according to its own course and laws, but he does not intervene in it, he does not intercede, he does not take over the work of a worldly cause, he supersedes nothing, he eliminates nothing. This does not mean, however, that we must deny any new initiative on God's part. His providence says precisely that he leads the world for us to the best advantage—and especially leads us in this world. But this leading in a certain direction by a certain initiative need by no means entail intervention. I can by virtue of my own free will move my arm, but in doing so my personal freedom in no way takes the place of the biochemical reactions which cause this movement. My person does not stand aside from these organic factors, cannot be added to it, replaces none of them, but rules them by permeating them. This is a weak simile for God's rule of the world. As ruling, guiding person—but utterly transcendent and at the same time more immanent than I am in my own body—he rules and guides the "body" of the world and gives

14. For an interpretation of the miracle stories from their insertion into the gospels, see Reginald H. Fuller, *Interpreting the Miracles*, London, 1966. The aspect of the possibility and the conditions of a (possible) miraculous event, however, remains still important; see P. Schoonenberg, *Covenant and Creation*, London, 1968, Chapter 4 and Epilogue.

in it to each being the being and doing proper to that being as its own. God does not compete; on the contrary, everything he does he gives us to do. This is true also in our human world and its history.

In contrast to evolution, our history, both large and small-scale, is led by human *freedom*. History is the interplay between human decisions and the situations arising therefrom whereby we are invited to ever more humanity, can accept it but also decline it. Does the same hold true for the relation between the free decision of man and God's creative rule of the world? This is a question with which man has ever been concerned and launched the fierce disputes we discussed at the opening of the book. For Molinism human freedom does not tolerate inducements from God: for Molina God's rule is not causal with regard to the act of will itself, as also appears to be the case for Levinas and other modern thinkers. Now one can, of course, quarrel over the concept of "cause," over the suitability of applying it to God's creation and still more over the question from which pattern of causality such creation must be approached. That God realizes our free wills, however, even as our own free act, is difficult to deny, if one seriously believes that he is the Creator. On this point Molina's opponents were in the right. It is only the question of whether they conceived of God's causality sufficiently transcendentally and did not err by having God add something to our free will and its action. God does not intervene between us and our decision. He does not compete with our action, but realizes it in the profound way in which it is ours, realizes it in its freedom. That this evokes a question concerning God's operations with regard to evil may present no difficulty, for on closer look it appears to hark back to the question: what is actually the reality of evil itself? Has evil as such a cause? In any case, where good is concerned God's creative causality extends to our freedom itself. God realizes this always, without in the least depriving us of our own decision.

What is valid for human freedom is also valid for its *norms*. Here too there is no "competition," from God, for just as he realizes our decisions as emanating from ourselves, so he also gives norms that derive from our own reality. That Yahweh hands over the tablets of the law to Moses is a great symbol of the fact that he also assumes the norms recognized by this people into his covenant. In the New Testament Jesus gives no laws, but presupposes them and interiorizes them. And the Holy Spirit dictates no laws, but gives us light and love to discover and set up norms of behavior. Here, however, it may still be noted that such norms do not merely illuminate from nature as opposed to the human person and human culture—just as God is not to be found only in "God's free nature." It is much more from the reality of ourselves as human persons in our mutual relationships that the norms are recognized as the demands of God.

GOD'S INITIATIVE

Until now we have been concerned mainly with denying God's intervention and assigning worldly causes in its place. This entails the by no means illusory danger of God disappearing behind the earthly in our minds, of seeming to be swallowed up in it, as the soul, the self, or the all of the world. On the other hand, we are called upon by the scriptures to affirm the radical transcendence and personal sovereignty of the Creator: "He spoke, and it came to be; he commanded and it stood forth" (Psalm 33, 9). The Church can never find God superfluous, can never let him be swallowed up in the world or even make him one of its attributes. The rejection of any kind of pantheism by the first Vatican Council (DS 3024) still holds today. This does not detract from what I said above, for this transcendence and sovereignty lie already included in God's positing of earthly reality. It is not the case that to God's immanence there should now be added his transcendence. Rather, it is precisely because of his transcendence that he does not stand beside a worldly cause, and is immanent in all cause and in all reality. From the point of view of the world, God's place cannot be empirically defined; but metaphysical reflection on its constant becoming, on the interaction of complementary causes, on the complexity of all earthly reality, shows us this as borne by and participating in the unlimited fullness-of-being. This thought is a complicated process in everyone and in humanity, but it leads us from and in the world to its origin, from and in the coherence of earthly causes to God's initiative.

This initiative of the Creator can encounter us most eloquently where the higher originates from the lower, where a considerable leap in evolution can be noticed, especially regarding the origin of

27

man. The special nature of such leaps is heightened still further by the fact that in all probability they are not carried out in a completely determined and necessary way. Evolution at least was able to carry out its substantial leaps in a different way. That this is also the case for the origin of man can appear from the fact that infrahuman nature is not automatically geared to man but must be conquered or forced open, that the humanization of this nature demands considerable effort.[15] In human history itself, with all respect for modern psychological and sociological findings, a complete determination of all events must be denied on the basis of human freedom. It is true that the choice between doing and not doing, between doing this or that, is not the most profound realization of our freedom, but it is nevertheless a realization which may not be denied, if we are actually free for the humanization of the chaotic situations which we encounter within and without ourselves. Thus there are always in human and infrahuman happenings points on which some things happen which could also have happened differently. If on these points the world truly comes to its completion, then there the initiative of the Creator is encountering us with special eloquence.

Here, however, there are two things which may not be forgotten. First, that here too the Creator adds nothing from outside. The higher arises truly and wholly from the lower and this lower is truly and wholly the cause and matrix for the higher. In the course of human history man is always active himself through his freedom or perhaps through the explosion of his determinisms. In the physical component of the miracle too nature shows, especially the biological nature of man himself, its openness for the movements of our freedom under God's grace. Even the clearest initiative from God does not complement, but leads the world itself to its optimum activation. Thus also a second thing becomes clear, that God's initiative is not limited only to the above significant cases. This exposition would be totally misunderstood if it were viewed as an attempt to exclude God from the common course of the world, reserving for him only a few special cases. Then the dilemma "God or world" would not be overcome. Rather, everything is to be explained by factors within the world, but in the coming into effect of these

15. A. G. M. van Melsen, *Evolution and Philosophy*, New York, 1965.

factors God has the initiative, he *is* the initiative. This is precisely what the words "God is Creator" mean.

Speaking of the creation, we can use various analogies or images by which the relation between the Creator and his world can be understood. The most common is, of course, that the Creator is seen as effective cause, maker, or artist. Precisely because this must be comprehended completely analogously or even metaphorically,[16] yet another comparison may be ventured. The Creator can also be called the soul, substance, or "self" of the world, so that the world is seen as God's embodiment. It is not only from outside Catholic thought that we receive such images. Even St. Thomas once ventured the same comparison: "In his rule God stands in relation to the whole universe as the soul stands in relation to the body."[17] Of God's transcendence it is clear that this comparison is to be understood metaphorically, but it is in the fact that the Creator precisely transcends all our barriers and is immanent in everything that the truth of the person-body comparison lies. As man as free person controls his body from within, thus too the Creator controls his creation from within. And as we as person move our body through free initiative, work with it and make it the expression of our being-person, without our free will adding anything to the biochemical factors which, for example, are responsible for a certain muscular movement, thus also the Creator moves and guides his creation through free initiatives which add nothing to the world, yet realize it.

It is obvious that here all the dependence which our person has with regard to our body must be excluded from our considerations. We are not a person without our body, not in our origin and not in all our earthly life—and probably not in all our existence; now and for ever; we are for that reason also person partly *through* our body. This, however, cannot be said of God: even if we cannot think of him without the world, we must in the same thought yet affirm that he exists through and from himself and in no way at all through the world. Thus although the analogy cannot be continued to the point of dependence which the person has with regard to his body, yet it

16. F. J. A. de Grijs, *Goddelijk mensontwerp. Een thematische studie over het beeld Gods in de mens volgens het scriptum van Thomas van Aquine,* Hilversum, 1967, pp. 430–433: criticism on the metaphor of the "artifex."

17. In *II Sent.,* dist. I, q. I, ad I.

nevertheless holds for the way in which the person "precedes" the body as initiative. The person shares his decision with the body, he gives it function and meaning—while at the same time a reverse relation arises—and thus the person is in his freedom, with his initiatives for his body in all dependence at the same time a transcendent living principle—another reason why even in an evolutionist outlook on man the unity of both is not that of a complete identity. This transcendence as source and initiative is, however, complete in God. He works in and behind the world, but we wrong the creative relation if we do not add that he is "above" and "before" the world. Our metaphysical reflection sees the world and all its happenings as participating in him;[18] in the encounter with God in our own existence and in history we experience him as guiding and calling.

Precisely for this reason the comparison of God with our embodied person does not appear so far removed from scripture as at first sight. Added to this is the fact that we find in the Bible itself a process of thought moving in this direction. After the anthropomorphic nearness of God in Yahwist soteriology and beside the inaccessible transcendence of the God who merely works through his angels, there comes in the Wisdom literature of the last centuries before Christ the thought of God's word, law, or wisdom which fulfills the universe. Wisdom especially is described as with God before the world, but on the other hand as related to his creation. It is born of God or created by Him before everything that is on earth, even before the abyss or chaos; it stands at the beginning of his path; together with God it makes and orders everything that is in heaven and earth (Proverbs 8, 22–36; Wisdom 7, 22–8, 1; Ecclesiastes 1, 4–10; 24; Baruch 3, 32–4, 4). Or more generally still: through wisdom God creates not only in the beginning, but he continues to impart life—that is, in scripture, the completion of all being, especially the human. Thus the wisdom of God is coupled with power and regulation. Especially with man, God, through his wisdom, is continuously giving life, and thus wisdom becomes the light for mind and heart. Because of this function for the whole of creation

18. For a justification of the doctrine of participation see H. Berger, *Op zoek naar identiteit. Het aristotelische substantiebegrip en de mogelijkheid van een hedendaagse metafysiek*, Nijmegen, 1968, pp. 177–190.

wisdom is also identified with the law, both with the law of exist-ence of things and the law of the covenant, the keeping of which is life for the Jew. Just like law, wisdom is especially granted to Israel while the other peoples do not know it. The wisdom which was in God's eternal tabernacle took root among the chosen people.[19] This thought process is also adapted, in the prologue to St. John's gospel, to God's Word, and there that Word concretized itself not only as light for mankind and for God's people—"his own"—but became flesh in Jesus Christ. In this Wisdom literature and its continua-tion in the New Testament we find thus that God guides his crea-tion from within, illuminates and awakens it to life. God precedes his people in the exodus event, which in the book of Wisdom (18, 15) is ascribed to his Word. The remarkable thing, however, is that wisdom, word, or law are on the one hand characteristics of God, but on the other hand as personified are distinguished in that they ema-nate from him, and that the word in the New Testament as become flesh in Jesus stands in dialogue with God. This brings us to the dia-logue of grace between God and man.

Before discussing this point it would be well once again to ascer-tain how much our pronouncements on the relation between God and his creation are and remain a continuous endeavor. No problem is being solved here, on the contrary we are approaching a mystery. We believe that we have gotten a false problem, a false dilemma, out of the way, but precisely this opens the prospect on to a mys-tery. Molinism and Báñezianism are surmounted; it appears that both of them in a one-sided way brought forward a certain truth: Molinism that of our own free causality, Báñezianism that of God's total causality. The supposition common to both, that God and world, God and man "compete," that their operations take place side by side, must be surmounted by the view that the Creator always gives to his creature the latter's own being and activity pre-cisely as his own. This view, however, appeared at the same time to include God's transcendent initiative, which we attempted to express by saying that the Creator is not absorbed by his creatures, but remains hidden behind them, and also precedes them in their actions. Even the false presupposition common to both systems seems to point to a truth. God does not work apart from "other" causes, nor

19. A. Hulsbosch, *God's Creation*, New York and London, 1965.

31

beside them, nor in competition with them, but he is ever present as the greater, the "earlier," as source and initiative. He is present not beside, but before and even above the creature; but this "before" and "above" must not place him outside and beside them. Mysteries usually express themselves in two propositions both of which we must affirm, but whose unity is always a question. The isolation of two propositions, insofar as these have taken place with Báñez and Molina, have been surmounted, but again in order to find in a different way two aspects of the same attitude of God, that is, immanence and initiative.

"NATURE AND GRACE"

In discussing now the relation between God and man by virtue of grace, we are not entering totally new territory. It is true that this relation is called "supernatural," and this term suggests that we are entering a higher level of reality. But what has just been said holds true not only for a "natural" relation, it holds for the whole relation of world and man to God. If the above is correct, then it also holds true for grace. If on the contrary the same cannot be said of grace, then the above was not correct or had merely limited validity. For that reason we shall now investigate whether in the grace-relation between God and man it also happens that God's initiative comes to us merely in the world, thus primarily in man. The term "supernatural" could indicate that this is not the case. On the other hand, God's concrete grace comes to us often, at least in relation to a fellow man and probably always in connection with the man Jesus Christ. Precisely here, however, the supernatural or unmerited initiative of God, bearing the name of election, predestination, or vocation, meets us perhaps in a greater way. But first let us consider the supernatural character of grace.

We begin with the question of whether the difference between nature and grace has any meaning. The terms in which it is expressed, the words "nature," "supernature," and "supernatural" are themselves just as open to discussion as the subsequent elaboration of the mutual relations between nature and grace. Even the concrete content of these terms cannot simply be chemically ascertained in view of the fact that man in his "nature" always stands in some relation to God's grace, receptive or otherwise. Yet the difference itself is in one way certainly based on God's act of salvation. God gives us still greater gifts than that of creation *for so far* as this coincides with our own capacities and operation. I still think that here the "covenant" is the most fundamental category, because God is not only foundation and source thereby, but associate of man, the latter's partner in dialogue. This already entails that God, like man, appear free and giving, and it thus supposes man, who is completely creature, in his own being and freedom. This giving is, however, a completely divine giving, a pure giving, that rests not on our worthiness or lovableness, but on God's election. "You did not choose me, but I chose you," says Jesus in the New Testament (John 15, 16), but these words can at the same time serve as a summary of what God intends for his people in the Old Testament. The same God has, as Father of Jesus, predestined us to his image, called and justified us (Romans 8, 29f.). These words indicate a loving initiative of God, ever desiring to grant salvation to all and realizing this in the highest way in Jesus Christ, in whom he places himself definitively present before us. Man is created to all this, is essentially and inwardly directed to this gift, which nevertheless remains wholly a gift. The term "supernatural" can suggest a division of two structures and for that reason I avoid it. Such terms, however, as "grace," "gift," and "unmeritedness" seem unavoidable, and furthermore the first two can be traced back to Scripture.

Concerning the further elaboration of the relation between God's gift of grace and man, I should still like to range myself on the side of St. Thomas, who has been rediscovered in this century by many authors, among whom Henri de Lubac deserves pride of place.[20] It is a matter here of the whole paradox of an absolute orientation towards, and an unconditioned desire for, a real goal—a *finis naturae* —which can, however, only be realized as a gift from God—which *excedit vires naturae*. The elaboration of this point we leave to de Lubac; here I should only like to raise a few questions on the distinction itself. First of all, does the distinction still have meaning? If the human subject that receives God's gift of grace, the human

20. His finest publication being *The Mystery of the Supernatural*, New York and London, 1967.

"nature" in the theological meaning of the word, is oriented wholly to those gifts, has a desire for these gifts, is it still meaningful to distinguish the subject from gift? To this one can again reply that the distinction cannot have the intention of tracing boundaries between the concrete reality of nature and the gifts of grace: this does not even appear possible anywhere where two realities pervade one another as respectively perfecting and receptive—as *actus* and *potentia*. The distinction is an expression of the unmeritedness, the grace or gift character of grace and of the fact that grace is given precisely for man as existing concretely. For that reason the distinction between grace and nature cannot be simply classed as only yet another distinction. In other words, for that reason grace remains unmerited for none other than for the existing man as such[21]

21. The unmeritedness of grace is related to something other than the existing nature of man as such primarily in two ways:

1. As general trend in the theology of the Reformation and in Baianism and Jansenism we encounter the concept that God's gifts are unmerited only for the man *fallen* in sin. The gifts of grace restore the man to an original condition in which, according to Baius in particular, the realities which are now ours by virtue of grace were merited to our nature as requirements for its own connatural purity. Concerning such a concept it must be acknowledged that the grace that we are aware of is indeed a gift of redemption, bestowed on us in an existence which is marked by sin. It is a question, however, of whether the unmeritedness of grace only holds in relation to the sinful element in our existence or with relation to our manhood as such. (This is the meaning of the question of whether the gifts of grace were unmerited for Adam in his first innocence. A clear view on the beginning of our race is not given us, as is today generally assumed, not even in scripture. For that reason it is better to formulate the question as above.) Insofar as grace is given to man as sinful, it pre-supposes sin; if it is given exclusively to sinful man, then grace presupposes sin without, conversely, sin presupposing grace. But this is precisely the case. Scripture always depicts sin as a break in the covenant, and this even holds for the "first" sin in Genesis 3, for "man" in Genesis 2 is described as completely in covenant with God (only the word "covenant" is lacking). Here too it is a matter of grace, of a giving—and demanding —encounter of God, of unmerited gifts. For that reason the classical concept that grace precedes sin still seems the best, although it seems to us now that we do not know anything of the historical way in which it preceded and that it might possibly be conceived as merely a logical presuppo-sition—as "*natura sed non tempore prius.*" Thus although the grace-nature relation appears to be accessible for us, merely in the grace-sin relation, it nevertheless lies at the foundation of the latter, and not vice versa. One can for that matter ask oneself why sin is made good by a merciful act of covenant of God, if it does not take place within a covenant-relation

But why the do nature and grace still have to be distinguished? Is this distinction not rendered invalid, seeing that world and man seem to be included in an evolving creation? Where then is a clearly defined nature against which one could limit grace as supernatural? The nature of all living is, seen from a great distance, always in process of development to higher forms; and this is valid even of the lifeless, which for that reason could rather be called the pre-vital. The nature of man is given into his own hands, the

---

with him. Then it could also be rectified by such an act of creation that man, by his own powers, rectifies what he has spoiled by his own action.

2. A second reduction of the difference between grace and nature conceives the latter term completely abstractly. It is no longer a matter of the nature of the existing man, let alone of that of the existing man in sin, but of the essence of the man without his concrete orientation to the gift of grace. To put it in technical terms: grace is seen in this concept as unmerited not with regard to the *"natura lapsa"* (the fallen man), nor with regard to the *"natura integra"* (the human nature apart from the influence of sin), but with regard to the *"natura pura"* (human nature apart from its appointed orientation to grace and blessedness). The concept indicated here is based on the fact that man in fact receives grace from God, but that he *could* also exist without this gift. This implies, however, that man is in fact inwardly oriented to God's gift of grace in his nature or in his essence, that he requires it, but that he could also exist without this orientation, in a "chemically pure" human nature, the above-named *"natura pura."* For most theologians who make a distinction between the nature which receives grace and the "natura pura" the orientation to grace is not internal, so that the difference between the two remains merely extrinsic. Here the man in the *"natura pura"* differs from that in the *"natura lapsa" "tamquam nudus a nudato"* (while from an existential view "naked" and "undressed" also entail an internal difference). However, if one conceives the difference between the hypothetical man who has nothing to do with grace and the existing man who is oriented towards it as an internal difference, then there is a possibility of regarding grace as unmerited merely for the former, while the really existing man with his orientation would also have a certain right to grace. There are past and present theologians who express this view (P. Smulders, *"De oorsprong van de theorie der zuivere natuur,"* in *Bijdragen* 10 [1949], 105–126; p. 125, in note 22: ". . . our concretely existing nature is exalted nature, is in fact destined by God for the beholding of God, so that it has no other concrete final aim; it has at the same time though an exigency with regard to the beholding of God."). Their position entails that the unmeritedness of which scripture and tradition speak falls totally outside the territory with which scripture and tradition are concerned, that is, the real man, and that the covenant of God is grace and election only for a hypothetical man. In this way the reality is taken from God's elective grace and thus also from the interpersonal relation in his covenant.

culture of yesterday is the nature of today. Can this not also be said of grace? That to which initially only grace enabled us can, if we accept it, become our personal attitude; in the terminology of the doctrine of virtue, it could be said that the *habitus infusus* becomes the *habitus acquisitus,* the infused virtue becomes personally acquired. In community life we see this clearly when what was given yesterday from charity—that is, from benevolence or mercy —is today the legal right of all. The grace of yesterday seems to have become the nature of today. All of this only affirms what was pointed out above, that no concrete frontier can be drawn between nature and grace. It does not, however, exclude the fact that grace remains a gift. The education of yesterday is also one's own attitude of today, but this does not exclude the fact that once one had to be educated. Thus it is also with regard to God as giver of grace. As Creator he gives us (just like our parents, but in his case completely from himself) a being that we do not receive, in view of the fact that it constitutes us as receiving. Moreover, God is in grace someone who encounters and presupposes our person as already existent: precisely this modality of dialogue or covenant indicates the special nature of the grace relationship within the creation relationship. The latter can, however, as a whole be understood only in a figurative sense as union or dialogue, as it does not presuppose anything of the creature. But where the proper covenant relation appears, the given becomes on the one hand ever more man's own being, while on the other hand it remains a gift and can be recognized more and more as gift. It is peculiar to thankfulness that what one has become oneself belongs to the other.

If we see the relation between nature and grace thus, then it accords completely with the view of man as occupying the summit of the evolving world. If we investigate the analogy between man and the infrahuman on all points, then it seems justified to include therein the nature-grace relation. One would then be able to compare the possibility of the lower forms rising to a higher form, the possibility of the primates becoming man, and on the other hand the realization of this possibility, the real manhood, for example, with the relation between nature and grace within the human world. It is self-evident that here we are discussing a distant analogy in the elaboration of which all points of difference must be acknowledged.

36

Two points in particular come under consideration. First of all, in man evolution has arrived at a being that consciously comprehends itself and constructs itself in freedom. Thus in man evolution does not progress as development of man to a different being, but of man to himself; one can say: not as mutation but as identification. Eternal life can rightly be contrasted with earthly life, but then as completion of the man himself, thus destined for every person and in such a way that each decides on his own fate. This completion lies certainly on the other side of death, because nothing that we now have and are can escape death. The new way of existence behind the frontier of death can then be regarded as a new nature of the same person, a concept which Hulsbosch elaborates very well. In itself, however, such a continued existence need not mean completion. It is only so because God gives himself in it, because covenant and dialogue here find their completion in knowing as we are known, in seeing face to face (1 Corinthians 13, 12). Only this self-giving of God, begun in life, makes the full reality of grace. It is not the giving of God's constant creation in general, not even that of the constant creating of man in general, nor even that of the perpetuation of the human person after death; it is precisely the encounter in which God gives himself to man as he already exists that constitutes grace.

If the difficulty of drawing a line between nature and gifts of grace were increased by our evolutive idea of the world, the actual unmeritedness of grace is not contradicted by it. On the contrary, this accords completely with such a picture of the creation. It accords particularly with the fact that in man evolution takes place freely. Herein the help of congeners, which among all living beings is received and given by the individual, is a help freely given and accepted in growing freedom: the instincts of mother and child are oriented towards a dialogue of love. This is not merely a superstructure over the animal in man: his instinctive life shows an extreme plasticity precisely for inclusion in this dialogue, it does not develop outside it. One of the most eloquent expressions of it is to be found in the fact that the human child must still learn all the patterns of movement with which the young animal is equipped from birth.[22]

22. A Portmann, *Biologische Fragmente zu einer Lehre vom Menschen,* Basel, 1961.

Thus man shows himself as a nature most profoundly defined by its openness—or undefined because of its openness—for the gift of others. The dialectics of a natural longing for an unmerited gift, of a desire for what can only be gift and be desired as gift, is proper to man; it almost forms his definition. The *desiderium naturale in finem quae excedit vires naturae* thus fits very well into an evolutive idea of the world. It was already ascertained by St. Thomas and the great scholastics of his time, with an improvement on Aristotle, that human nature differs from that of the infrahumans in that the latter can achieve their aim by their own powers and man cannot. Man is a higher being, so says Thomas in particular, because it is more perfect to achieve a higher goal not by one's own power than to achieve a lower goal by them.[23] This scholastic thesis, which supposes a divine aid, is supported by what has just been said on interhuman aid. Thus it appears to lie wholly in the line of evolution that man is a being open to unmerited, bestowed help and fulfillment, from his fellow men and ultimately from God himself. Whereby it should still be noted that this openness for fulfillment does not allow us to decide outside revelation on the reality or even on the distinct possibility of grace and eternal life. Only the fulfillment of the natural longing reveals to us its most profound orientation.

GOD AND MAN IN GRACE

I thought it useful to make these observations on the meaning of the gift character of grace before raising the question of how far God and man also collaborate in the grace relation. The term "supernatural" seems to indicate what is brought about by God alone, vertically onto interhuman relations. But the words "unmerited," "gift," and so forth indicate human relations as a point of comparison. Would it, moreover, not be true to say that precisely *in* the encounter between man and man, God bestows his grace? Would this perhaps be necessary in the same way as with the above described realization of earthly effects in general?

23. *Summa theol.* I II, q. 5, a. 5, ad 2: ". . . *creatura rationalis, quae potest consequi perfectum beatitudinis bonum, indigens ad hoc divino auxilio, est perfectior quam creatura irrationalis quae huiusmodi boni non est capax, sed quoddam bonum imperfectum consequitur virtute suae naturae.*"

To these questions one could probably answer first of all that it is so *in fact*. In all grace human mediation is conceivable. God bestows on us his gift of grace through the "one mediator between God and men, the *man* Christ Jesus" (1 Timothy 2, 5): not merely because of his merits but also because "from his fullness have we all received" (John 1, 16). This certainly holds within the community of grace which is Christ's Church, in which, in addition, moreover Christ perpetuates himself as "sacrament of the encounter with God" in the other forms of sacramentality and mediation of salvation. But it is also generally assumed of God's extra-ecclesial and pre-Christian salvific dispensation that it belongs to a plan of salvation that achieves its completion in Christ. This orientation to the God-*man* should not be conceived as limited to our race insofar as it is fallen into sin. It is much rather present in all humanity and all the cosmos, for "in him all things hold together" (Colossians 1, 17). The Scotist outlook on the general mediatorship of the word become flesh was also taken up later in Thomist thought and has thus found a broad recognition. Of course, Christ's mediation seems to be universal in the order of final causality rather than in that of effective causality: the "through him" must be explained by the "for him" or "to him." But perhaps too a certain parallel can be concluded from all this: if God's salvific dispensation is oriented to mediation by the man Jesus, will it not then already before Jesus occur through human mediation? If this is the case, the mediatorship of this Man would appear to be an inner crowning of what is oriented towards him. Classical theology touched on this thought in its speculations on the influence of Adam. What Adam caused for all men in evil is the reverse side of what he could and had to bring about in good. If he has played a part which deprives us of God's gift of grace, then he has been called to mediate for us in the obtaining of these gifts. Adam's position is expounded in scholasticism in all sorts of ways, ultra-realistically and purely juridically. If it is understood according to the ways in which parents influence their children and in general in the way in which one man influences another morally and religiously, then an analogous Adam role can be assumed for all, and that of the first man is perhaps not so special as classical theology conceives it.[24] Thus we

24. P. Schoonenberg, *Man and Sin*, Notre Dame, 1968, Chapters 3 and 4 and esp. pp. 177–191: "Original Sin and the Sin of the World."

come through Adam just as through Christ to a general mediation of grace of man for man. It is already on the basis of these considerations that one can speak, as do modern theologians, about the "sacrament of the brother"[25] and call the brotherhood of man the "sacrament of God's universal salvific will."[26] In all probability God's dispensation of grace appears in fact to be always mediated by men.

Greater certainty can be awarded the above if we also affirm that it *must* be so. Indeed, such a view forces itself upon one. Based on what has been said above in general on the concurrence of God and worldly cause, the question can also be raised whether it could be otherwise than that in grace also God works by using man as mediator. It is precisely the unmerited nature of the gifts which leads us to this question. How can it be that the ever and everywhere creating God appears now as the ally of man, the Ground as "over against"? How can he, from whom man is, still in the strict sense give to man? How can God make himself present in this new way for and in man, where He is already present in all dimensions of his creation? How can God realize something that is completely from himself but not completely from man? Something that man himself does not produce through God's total causality, but to which he is purely receptive? We have already ascertained that man to man can stand in a receptive relationship. It is then obvious that God in this bestowing, in which he is a Partner for the man created by himself, utilizes a man-to-man relationship, that he bestows grace on man through fellow man.

This can be affirmed still more by formulating our conclusion of the beginning in a different way. The fact that within the world *definite* beings arise, *definite* events take place, *definite* relations arise, can never be explaind from God alone, but from God and a worldly cause, from God as the one who realizes a worldly cause. The writer of the book of Joshua (10, 11) describes a heavy hailstorm by saying that Yahweh cast down stones; in the book of Job (38, 22) God knows the storehouses of hail: the second is a completion of the first. Galaxies

25. H. U. von Balthasar, *The God Question and Modern Man*, New York, 1967, pp. 142–155: "The Sacrament of the Brother."
26. B. Langemeyer, "Sündenvergebung und Brüderlichkeit," in *Catholica* 18 (1964), 290–314; p. 305: "*Die Mitmenschlichkeit könnte man . . . das Sakrament des allgemeinen Heilswillens Gottes nennen.*"

and snowflakes, rockets and human children, they never come exclusively from God but from God and world, God and man. Of the examples given no one will dissent, but it is also generally valid. The diversity within creation indeed finds its source in God, but only insofar as God makes the worldly causes themselves produce the effects peculiar to them, insofar as he, by means of worldly factors, causes worldly relations to arise. Now this also holds for the reality which we call gift of grace or relation of grace. This also God brings about by introducing another creature. And as God is giving in grace, so this creature can only be the other man, for only men can give one another something and themselves. For that reason, if God gives us his supernatural grace, this can only happen by his directing us to one another as giving men. The fact just ascertained, that the God-man and each fellow man is a sacrament of divine encounter, appears to rest on necessity. Only in the other man, in his giving relation to me and in my giving relation to him, does God's grace stand before me as giving.

Theological views do not raise from glib assertions. We must go still further and take into account a contrary conception, or at least a real question. These arise from experience. Is it always the case that God is giving to us in a giving fellow man? Certainly, his grace coming to us in the giving gesture of a loving person is a real experience, but oftener still we will experience grace as a call to give love to others, even to forgive others. The sacrament of the divine encounter is not merely the man who enriches us through his love, it is more still the widow and the orphan, the deprived and stricken man we encounter along life's path, even the foe whom we must love. Grace is not only a blissful receiving, it is much more the mission to a giving which is more joyful than receiving. This experience we find affirmed in the history of salvation, in the prophets and apostles. God's grace does not come to them—at least not at first sight—through fellow men, but this grace sends them precisely to fellow men who, poor and even devoid of grace, enter their life. And this is certainly and surely the case with Jesus Christ. He is sent to us by the Father, not vice versa. If he calls us those "whom thou hast given me" (John 7, 2), then we are only given to him as the receivers, as the people that he acquires, as those whom he takes from poverty to riches, even from death to life. But then is not the argument that God gives in a giving man refuted by innumerable facts? Is not God's grace the mission to receive men, is it not more this than an encounter with giving men, is it not this mission to receive men especially in its culmination?

All these questions are certainly real. But must they for that reason overthrow the necessity of the human role in any dispensation of grace? For the fact that God's grace primarily leads us to an asking and not to a giving fellow man must be fully recognized. Whether a giving man does not come into grace in any way is, however, still to be seen. First of all, there is the man himself who appeals to us. He shows us the possibilities of our own heart, and this confers a benefit, for giving is blessed. His role of asking may soon change, and we can even expect it. Moreover, how did we become susceptible to the call that this man places upon us? Was it not because we ourselves have already encountered a giving man, have received from him or at least have been encouraged and liberated to giving by his example? Through the mediation of giving men the giving to which I am now called has become a value for me, through them the grace to give now has been mediated. The contradistinction between giving and receiving does not seem to be absolute; God in his grace has given us to one another, and sometimes with each of us our role is active and then passive, and always changing.

In this perspective faith leads us further. It shows us Jesus Christ as the totally giving man, who, however, identifies with the man whom we must feed, clothe, care for, and comfort, whose loneliness we may fill, to whom we may give ourselves (Matthew 25, 31–46). This means more specifically that he is present in their appeal as the power to give. We are all a demand for one another, but the possibility of always giving becomes, through Jesus Christ, present in the human race. Finally, he who is purely the Man for others enables us to give for one another.

It will be worth while to elaborate this point further. Existentially, we are always referred from the asking to the giving man, and ultimately to Christ. The asking man in our life wishes to be our neighbor and we may and must be so for him, but his appeal penetrates with much difficulty. Our morals are so often like the "enclosed morals" described by Bergson, that cannot see beyond the frontiers of our particular environment, or hear an appeal coming from afar. What if the frontiers were fixed by enmity and if the other has also become obdurate? Can we then understand the call that lies in that other as fellow man, without his first having made peace with us? Jesus has made note of such "enclosed morals": "You have heard that it was said: You shall love your neighbor and hate your enemy" (Matthew 5, 43). Only he could command to love the enemy too, because only he has opened the way to it in our race through his love "to the end" (John 13, 1) for those who were "his own" and for those who repudiate him. The love without frontiers and conditions had already begun to be preached in the Old Testament. Not only those from whom we may expect something or those who are of our race, says Deuteronomy (24, 17–22) may ask us for our aid, but also the "widow and the fatherless and the sojourner within your towns." The prophets also preach this love, and place it above worship. "So whatever you wish that men would do to you, do so to them: for this is the law and the prophets" (Matthew 7, 12). But this great appeal of the Old Testament, doing away in principle with enclosed morals and declaring piety worthless without love of one's neighbor, still calls for the Man in whom it becomes reality. In him grace appears victorious. It is for this reason that Paul feels so sharply the contrast between law and grace, that he sees in the law merely impotence and thus the stimulus to sin, and experiences in Christ primarily freedom from the law. For Matthew, who is more aware that the law is always included in the covenant and as such brings salvation, Christ brings the fulfillment of the law itself (5, 17).

GOD'S INITIATIVE IN GRACE

Thus we have seen that where at first sight God's grace does not meet man in a giving man, such a man is not, however, lacking. But all this cannot undo the moment of calling or mission and thus of God's initiative. Perhaps each of us, but certainly the prophets and most of all Jesus, experience the realization that they are sent from God to mankind, that there lies a moment in their grace that is not mediated by man. This moment has until now been described as a calling prepared within human relations but subsequently transcending them. The transcendence can, however, have already been present in the beginning. The initiative of God that lifts the called above human relations can already be prepared in the "anticipating grace" through which a whole previous human upbringing can only be understood as this appeal of God. Thus it is conceivable that in an upbringing in which reference to God, and even one in which the brotherhood of man, was partially lacking, these concepts can be assimilated later as corrective. It has a profound meaning when Jeremiah and John the Baptist are said to be called "from the womb." In a totally unique way this is true for Jesus Christ. God's sharing of grace meets him without his having preceded the encounter in any way whatever—neither with priority of time nor even of nature. Thus God embraces the human existence of Jesus in all its dimensions, even in its origins. We must then take into account in this man, but to a certain degree in every man, this moment of the outstripping or conquering element of grace. In the grace dialogue mediated by men there lies always a moment that surpasses mediation, that outstrips it. More still than in the general relation among creatures is God's initiative visible in grace.

In our discussion above on the relation between creator and creature in general, we saw that God's initiative does not contradict his cooperation with created causes, but rather is presupposed by such cooperation. Precisely because God activates the creature, the latter can be active both with regard to itself and with other creatures. What holds for creation as a whole holds in a special way for the covenant relationship within this creation. There precisely can the other for me, but I too for the other, be mediator of God's grace through vocation and mission. This is true to the highest degree in Jesus Christ. It must then be stressed that God's grace is primarily a force in the very one who is called and sent, a force of and in that man, which is why scholastic theology rightly speaks of created gifts of grace. Only thereby can the graced man mediate for the other. To this we can also add that even the openness for this mediation of grace of the other again presupposes a created gift of grace in him. We have just now used as point of departure the fact that it is always the fellow man, the other, who appears for oneself as mediating grace. Now we must add that, just as in the whole creation relationship, God's grace also brings about an immanent activity in man, and thus a direct answer. That we have just conceived of the grace relationship exclusively as one going beyond the other man is due to the fact that we have placed it in the covenant. In grace God himself is the Other, the partner, one's counterpart and Thou, and this he can only be through his immanence in another man who is a thou to oneself. Thus we should now like to extend our definition of the grace relationship. If we have defined it up to now as a covenant relation between God and man, now we should say: it is a covenant relation *with everything that this relation implies.* Biblically speaking, then: the covenant with the election it supposes and the mission to establish this covenant. This election is then real in the elected man, it is his power, his faith, hope, and love, everything that theology styles created gifts of grace.

This makes even clearer what we ascertained at the beginning: nature and grace are distinguishable from one another only in theory. Grace shows itself in the covenant relation, which is embodied in human solidarity; this relation is prepared in a vocation to God, which is at the same time a mission to others. Here we accept one of the main suppositions of Hulsbosch's book on the creation, that grace is not added to creation but has its place within it.[27] Everything that Hulsbosch says on grace, sin, and redemption he can rightly summarize under the title *God's Creation,* as also de Haes can write a book on *The Creation as Mystery of Salvation.*[28] That the grace relationship falls within creation need not conflict with classical theology either, as it too speaks of created gifts of grace: *gratia creata,* indicating thereby that the grace relationship always rests or coincides with a quality or way of being of and in the creature himself. Just as any relation between myself and another—if it is to be more than what a third party may say about me and this other—is a way of being of myself, so also is the relation which God gives me in his covenant. Scholasticism (partly as a defense against the concept present among some Reformation theologians of a purely forensic righteousness) even bestowed its full attention on the reality of sanctifying grace and called this—as also the synod of

27. Hulsbosch, *God's Creation* (note 19).
28. P. de Haes, *De schepping als heilsmysterie,* Tielt, 1962; see also by the same author, *Schepper en schepsel,* Tielt, 1967, pp. 9–18.

Dordrecht—a new quality in man. Although scholasticism's attention to this matter was something of a hindrance towards the recognition of the biblical and patristic view that it is primarily the Holy Spirit who is given to us, it nevertheless remains completely true that there is no residing of God nor any bond with God unless there is given at the same time an inner disposition of man, a created gift of grace. Through entering into a covenant with man and giving himself to him, God truly alters man (and we can add: thereby God also truly changes for and to man, but that is a different question). Mediation of grace is thus one of the ways in which God is creative, although a completely specific way. Perhaps scholasticism's exclusive attention to this individual nature of grace on the one hand, on the other its insufficiently comprehensive outlook on God's creation itself, hindered it from placing the grace relationship, the covenant, freely within the creation. I have done this myself in the past, but without further elaboration. This elaboration can be found on a generous scale in Hulsbosch's writings for whom, however, the concept of covenant remains unelaborated. In this connection the philosopher Levinas can again be made use of. While Hulsbosch does not give much individual relief to the covenant of grace within creation, and while Levinas on the other end reduces creation to the covenant, Levinas's categories seem serviceable in describing the peculiar nature of the covenant in Hulsbosch's view, but in such a way that God encounters man not merely through asking and demanding but also through giving, not merely in the law but primarily in Jesus Christ.

SALVATION HISTORY

The covenant of grace is included in God's creation. But the world created by God, at least the visible one, is a world in evolution—if we employ the term "evolution" for the time being very broadly and allow it to include history. Seen by its result—scholastically speaking: passive or terminative—God's creation *is* thus evolution and history. And God's covenant in it *is* salvific history. We shall now investigate this aspect of the covenant.

The first thing that strikes one here is that God's work is carried out *in* history, *in* the historicity of everything human, of Israel and of Jesus Christ himself. God's institutions are also human institutions. That means that they have arisen from a human pre-history and that they always entail the historical limitation of human works. Israel, the Church, and the sacraments are not from nothing. Israel is compared to a "wandering Aramaean" (Deuteronomy 26, 5), the Church is from Israel and the peoples, the Eucharist from Passover meal or chaburah, Christian baptism from that of John. And the realities which arose thus are on the one hand truly institutions of God, which for that reason continue in our history, and on the other hand they entail a historical limitation which not even their "nucleus" can ever be freed of, and they are thus always susceptible to reformation. For that reason the Church can alter the sacraments, though the Council of Trent cautions: "while retaining their substance" (DS 1728), but is wise enough not to describe this substance. The salvific realities exist "by virtue of divine law," but their form is always at the same time "of human law" and thus alterable; the border between both territories cannot be defined, and indeed cannot be defined in principle.

Thus God's revelation exists in the self-revelation of man as affected by the God of his salvation, indeed it *is* at the same time this human self-revelation. God's word exists in human words and *is* human words. Inspiration is for that reason not a divine dictation, but divine guidance of a human history of traditions and literary forms, just as the *assistentia* or aid of the Spirit does not exclude the seeking of the Church but actually activates it. Thus God's Spirit does not have a separate different meaning for a text other than that which lies in the text itself (the customary interpretation of the *sensus plenior*), but he gives the illumination through which the reality indicated by this text can be more profoundly discovered by rereading it in a new situation. In the same way the Spirit guides the translation of the old dogmas in a new situation, by introducing a new outlook on man and world and not by jealously watching over the mere letter. What the Holy Spirit brings about in the human element in the interpretation of revelation, he also brings about in the celebration of the sacraments. What Christ and the Spirit share in grace and what one man announces meaningfully to the other—in older terms: the working of grace and the psychological effect of preaching and sacraments—are two sides of the same activity. Transsubstantiation is not an intervention of God on the occasion of the *not so if you retain the term, "transubstantiation"*

priestly words of consecration, it is the realization of what bread and wine mean for Christ and those who may represent him. In eastern theology the divine Logos takes possession of the gifts of bread and wine; this is totally acceptable, provided we say here that the Logos does this in his human reality by going the way of human communication through bread and wine to the ultimate.

If we view the history of salvation more from the "inside angle," then we can see God's judgments as being at the same time man's determination of his own fate. God's reward and punishment is not an intervention from outside. Elsewhere we have pointed out at length how this is particularly valid for the punishment of sin.[29] Already in the course of the Old Testament God would appear to be conceived not only as the one who is angry at the sins of his people, but as jealous of their love and thus full of anxiety for their salvation. The punishment of sin is not the vengeance with which God retaliates but the misery, the alienation and impoverishment, the death that comes over man if he has forsaken his source of life. Especially in the book of Wisdom it is sin which itself creates disaster, which comes into the world through the envy of the devil, while God continues to have mercy on the man whom he has created to immortality (2, 23). In the New Testament we see in the epistle to the Romans how God's anger is revealed—provisionally, until the revelation of his redeeming righteousness—by leaving man to his own sin (1, 18–32). And in St. John, judgment is brought about now, but in the deeds and attitudes of man: he who believes has eternal life, he who hardens in unbelief will not see life (3, 18ff., 36).

That is to say that the eternal fate of man also lies in his own hands, or better still: in his own answer in his dialogue with God. The leap between this and the other life need in no way be denied: it can rightly be regarded as a crossing of a threshold in human evolution, as we elaborated above in connection with Hulsbosch's theory. But here at the same time a self-surpassing takes place: man in eternity is the result of his own determining of his position in time. The concept of "merits" must not then be understood too economically, and certainly not from within the framework of our financial economy. We do not barter our deeds for something else. The reward for a good deed is already on earth in the depths of our

29. P. Schoonenberg, *Man and Sin* (note 24), pp. 57–62.

being in the fact that we might do this deed, that it inalienably helps to determine our person and all our relations. In the most complete sense this holds for our eternal reward. But blessedness still remains a gift, to be ascribed to God's initiative. The grace by which we might do even the least good is already initiative and gift of God, and in all our merits he is crowning his own gifts, while on the other hand, as the Council of Trent says, God is so much a giving God that he makes his gifts our merits (DS 1548). But any growth, and certainly the blossoming of time to eternity, is also the initiative and gift of God, and the latter more than any other. It is birth through the tunnel of death, a rising from the dead, in which for scripture God creates in the most intense way and makes everything new.

Thus we arrive again at the initiative of God, this time his initiative in the history of salvation. One can say that all our history is salvific history just insofar as and because through God's initiatives it truly realizes progress. Insofar as these initiatives remain unanswered, human history is ambivalent: there is progress in one area —qualitative and, lacking that, quantitative—but this can always be used for or against love. Insofar as man opposes God's initiatives, he is establishing the history of evil, which is just as universally oppressive as the history of salvation is liberating: herein lies the whole secret of original sin. God's initiatives are consequently to be recognized everywhere that man is liberated to love, to the one love towards God and his fellow man. This is not necessarily to be found only in those places where "divine worship" or, more exactly, "religion," occurs or is more widespread, that is, where forms or institutions or even formulations arise which bring the relation between God and man to expression. These can, however, be signs of this relation—and are intended as such—but they can also, through our indolence and sinfulness, become empty, false, or misleading. The emergence of forms of divine worship in humanity is for that reason a provisional salvific *kairos,* full of promise and danger; the purifying of religion and its union with the true God-man relation in Israel is promise, but its completion in Jesus Christ is purely a gift.[30]

30. P. Schoonenberg, *God's World in the Making,* Pittsburgh and Dublin, 1965, Chapter III: "The History of Salvation."

II.

God and Man, or God in Man?

UNTIL recently, many Christians were brought up with the image of Jesus as being both God and man, the one Christ in two natures. This held for Roman Catholics, for the Orthodox of the Eastern Churches, and for broad sections of the Reformation Churches. Now this image is being called into question. This questioning could not for long remain restricted to the world of specialist theologians: this had already proved impossible when, in the nineteenth century, the liberal image of Jesus was disputed in the Reformation Churches, and it is even less possible today when modern communications make closed discussion in theology, as well as in any other science, nearly impossible. Perhaps the question, or even the negative answer, has even penetrated so far that many Christians, including many Catholics, no longer recognize their conviction in the image of Jesus as God and man. On the other hand, many others view the attacks on this image with profound dismay and pain. We are indeed concerned with the nucleus of our faith here. But this faith will not be saved by a tenacity which evades questions, just as little indeed by a reduction to personal taste of what has been handed down to us. The question is this: what does a real, creative loyalty to our faith in Jesus as the Christ demand? How can this faith be professed today without foreshortening and distortion, but also without holding onto patterns of thought which no longer express what was formerly intended?

Many publications over recent years have described the confession of Jesus Christ and Son of God as it is expressed in the holy scripture of the New Testament and in post-biblical tradition.[1] The

1. In recent years, New Testament christology has divided into studies

50

Christ-confession of tradition culminated to a certain degree in the doctrine of the Council of Chalcedon—the point of departure for classical christology in the Churches of East and West and also in the Reformation—namely, the christology of Jesus as being both God and man. Thus we shall take a very close look at Chalcedonian christology not only for the purpose of drawing new conclusions from it, but also and above all so that succeeding dogma may be united again with early tradition, with the christology of the New Testament, with the kerygma which lies at its foundation, and with the figure of Jesus himself, who meets us in this kerygma.

INTRODUCTION: THE CHALCEDONIAN PATTERN AND THE OBJECTIONS AGAINST IT

Patterns are always catalytic agents in our learning processes. Our intuitive contact with a specific reality is expressed in concepts and judgments which relate to our previous knowledge of a thing. Thus a more or less graphic pattern soon arises, a summary of already acquired knowledge which also, to a large extent, determines further investigation and question. Such patterns appear in our knowledge of all layers of reality, whether this knowledge is scientific or pre-scientific. The farmer speaks in a pre-scientific pattern of knowledge of nature when he says in the spring that "the cold must first come

---

which either concentrate on the titles ascribed to Jesus or pursue the various christological strands. Of the first we can cite: O. Cullmann, *The Christology of the New Testament,* Westminster, 1964; Ferdinand Hahn, *The Titles of Jesus in Christology,* London, 1969. Directly oriented to the strands are R. H. Fuller: *The Foundations of New Testament Christology,* New York and London, 1965; R. Schnackenburg, "Christologie des Neuen Testamentes," in *Mysterium Salutis III/1,* ed. by J. Feiner and M. Löhrer, Einsiedeln, 1969, pp. 227–383. Summaries of christology in the post-biblical tradition, at least until Chalcedon, are given in P. Smulders, "De ontwikkeling van het christologisch dogma," in *Bijdragen* 22 (1961), 357–422; J. Liébaert, "Christologie. Von der Apostolischen Zeit bis zum Konzil von Chalkedon," *Handbuch der Dogmengeschichte III/1a* Freiburg, 1965; J. N. D. Kelly, *Early Christian Doctrines,* New York and London, 1965, especially Chapters IV and IX–XII; A. Grillmeier, "Die theologische und sprachliche Vorbereitung der christologischen Formel von Chalkedon," in A. Grillmeier and H. Bacht, *Das Konzil von Chalkedon. Geschichte und Gegenwart I,* Würzburg, 1951, pp. 5–202; this study was later elaborated in A. Grillmeier, *Christ in Christian Tradition,* New York, 1965.

out of the ground"; groups think of other groups in patterns: the division between conservative and progressive is one example. The word "pattern" itself comes, so far as I know, from the natural sciences, which make frequent use of it. But psychology and sociology too work with patterns or types, as with "the authoritarian personality," or "the community of interests."

Patterns are useful and necessary, but they are also dangerous. They can lead questioning in the right but also in the wrong direction, and they can even thwart it at a given point, or misdirect us into unfruitful or harmful inquiry. In theology, for example, a too graphic and insufficiently thought-out pattern of the relation between God and man caused late scholastic thought to enter into a fruitless dispute over grace and free will, and this is today the cause of numerous misunderstandings concerning God among both atheists and theists. Thus we should state at the outset that we shall here have to answer first the question of how much the pattern of the two natures in Christ brings us closer to his reality, of how it may estrange us from the person of Jesus Christ.

The reader will, however, first ask himself whether it is justified, admissible even, in theology, and especially in christology, to speak of patterns. Let us limit the question to christology, for it forms the heart of theology and is bound up with the doctrine of the Trinity and with the whole question of salvation and salvific history. Is it possible and admissible, in connection with the mystery of Jesus Christ, to speak of patterns of thought? The fact that it has been done[2] does not, of course, constitute an answer to the question. Those who ask the question can point out the divine character of the act of faith, the content of which is made explicit in "sacred" theology; they can also point out the divine person of Christ himself. This, however, does not exclude the human element in believing, professing, and faith, nor the human recognizability of Christ. Faith is always a gift of the Holy Spirit, but it is at the same time and just as much a human decision and a human expression, de-

2. On the use of "patterns" or "models" in believing and theological discussion see in particular the works of Ian Ramsey: *Religious Language*, New York and London, 1957; and *Models and Mystery*, London, 1964. For the christological patterns see John McIntyre, *The Shape of Christology*, Westminster and London, 1966; John Knox, *The Humanity and Divinity of Christ. A Study of Patterns in Christology*, Cambridge, 1967.

termined by the history of the man who believes, the views which his world teaches him, the questions it poses to him. For that reason the Holy Spirit leads the Church to the full truth along the actual paths of human thought, and a truly believing theology need not be ashamed to recognize these paths in the past, and if necessary to improve them today. Indeed, God's Son, through his very recognizability as man, comes under our human patterns of thought. It is precisely the totally unique impression that his person makes on those who believe in him that required them to reach for familiar patterns—which, however, were transcended again and again.

These patterns were not simply general concepts. The patterns which were applied to Jesus from the Old Testament are also unique, in that they characterize a figure in which God's actions reaches fulfillment. This holds especially true for the titles "Son of God," "Servant of Yahweh," and "Son of man." The christology of the New Testament consists to a great extent in adapting these and similar given patterns to Jesus and at the same time in correcting and interconnecting them, as can be seen from the works of Cullman, Hahn, and Fuller. There is an interaction too between the patterns of Jewish and Hellenistic origin: the christological hymn of Philippians 2, 6–11, for example, depicts to a certain extent the earthly existence of Jesus in the image of the Servant, and the glorified life certainly in that of the Lord, while at the same time (showing a strongly Hellenistic influence) trying to make clear the relation of Jesus as Lord to God the Father. Not only the patterns of "Servant" and "Lord," but all christological titles, comprise an attempt to describe the relation of Jesus to God and at the same time to his fellow men. Moreover, the titles refer more or less to Jesus' own history, insofar as they are individually more suitable either for Jesus' earthly life and death, his return, or his constant presence in the Church.

The relation between earthly and glorified life is the theme of the gospels. In theological retrospection on the earthly life some patterns of thought can also be distinguished from the point of view of the glorification. An old strand in the kerygma says more or less clearly that Jesus, after his earthly life, especially on his rising from death, is appointed and made Lord, Messiah, and High Priest (Acts 2, 36; Romans 10, 9; Philippians 2, 9; Hebrews 1, 3f.; 5, 9f.). Even

53

Jesus' divine sonship is related with his resurrection (Acts 13, 33; Romans 1, 4; Hebrews 1, 5). One could then with some justification talk of an adoptionist pattern of thought. But this pattern is often modified in the context without its being abolished (as in Romans 1, 4: "Son of God in power"). Even the gospels as a whole, including the synoptics, refer to Jesus' unique relation to the Father in words from his earthly life (especially Matthew 12, 27 and par.). All narrate Jesus' baptism as his calling to be prophet, servant, and Son, but none of the evangelists can refrain from already announcing him previously as Messiah and Son of God. Mark does this merely in the titles which he acknowledges to Jesus in the first verse of his gospel; the others precede a narrative prologue to the material of the preaching of the twelve (Acts 1, 22): Matthew and Luke in the form of the history of Jesus' youth, John in the form of his pre-history as Word with the Father and in the world since the creation. Two patterns of thought here emerge by which any adoptionism is definitely surmounted: Jesus' origin is ascribed totally to God either through his conception from the Holy Spirit or through his pre-existence as Logos. Various authors have attempted to show the relativity of these two ideas by pointing out the very fact that they would be mutually exclusive. Certainly, these two patterns are not connected with one another within the New Testament, and they answer respectively to a pneuma and a Logos christology. There would be a contradiction, however, only if the virginal conception was a foundation of Jesus' divine sonship in the sense that He is the Son of God only from the moment of his conception in Mary's womb. But this is not stated in Luke 1, 35: the virginal origin of Jesus can also be understood there in that on the one hand it is reason for us to recognize Jesus as Son of the Most High, while on the other hand it is a result of Jesus' divine sonship or at least of his pre-existence as pneuma. Later tradition has thus done nothing unlawful in connecting both patterns of thought.

If we now pass from the biblical patterns of thought to that of classical christology, especially that inspired by Chalcedon, then we are entering a different world. The various biblical titles are in practice merged into one, that of "Son of God." In this title, furthermore, there is one aspect that is given strong elaboration, namely, that of union with the Father. This has come to mean oneness of divine being, through the adaptation of another of the above named patterns of thought, that of pre-existence. In the post-biblical tradition the Logos of the prologue to St. John's gospel becomes more and more the Son, already in his pre-existence, and thus a divine person with the Father. For Justin he is a spiritual force (λογικὴ δύναμις) who, in the Old Testament, appears in human form (*Dial. c. Tryph.,* 61), but from whom even heathen philosophers such as Socrates receive a part before he has become entirely the Christ (*Apol. sec.,* 10). Hippolytus, who fought against the identification of the Father and Christ, attributes an individuality to the Logos, but says on the other hand that "the Logos in itself and without the flesh was not completely Son" (*Contra haer. Noeti,* 15). For so far as the existence of the Logos before the incarnation was considered in the second and third centuries, its relation to the world and man has pre-eminence over that to the Father. Yet the Logos came more and more distinctly to be a person beside the Father, even in its pre-existence, due to the conflict over adoptionism and modalism and, above all, the whole of the pre-existence theology—or rather the pre-existence philosophy, for its inspiration is middle Platonism—of Origen. The Council of Nicea spoke in a theological framework influenced by the pre-existence speculations of Origen. Moreover, the Arianism repudiated by Nicea is itself a pre-existence concept: it regards the Logos which has become flesh in Jesus Christ as created, certainly, but at the same time as first-born and demiurge with regard to all other creatures. If in answer the Church upholds the biblical doctrine that in Jesus Christ "dwells the whole fullness of deity" (Colossians 2, 9), then in the given situation it would be difficult to express it other than by explaining the Logos wholly as the Son, who is one with the Father. The Nicene doctrine is in part contained in the closer definition of an existent baptism symbol (DS 125). But this results in the fact that everything said of the Son is ultimately awarded to the "Lord Jesus Christ," for "God's only begotten Son" is in opposition to this name. On the other hand, however, in the symbol of Nicea the whole union with the Father is named before the incarnation of the Son, so that the Son is described as person before his becoming man, albeit not without reference to "Jesus Christ." This pre-existence becomes clearer still because, in the canon added to the symbol, the origin of the Son is proposed as being beyond all time (DS 126);

55

and the first Council of Constantinople replaces the Nicean expression "begotten from the substance of the Father" with "begotten from the Father before all ages" (DS 150). From then on the pre-existence of the Son came to control christological belief and thought.

In a christology not ruled by this personal pre-existence, two types are already possible, one emphasizing Jesus' being-man and the other seeing him primarily as "from God" and "not from here." We can call them respectively an adoption and an incarnation christology. In the second century these types found their most extreme exponents in Ebionitism and Docetism. These two christological conceptions can be regarded as the intensification of two types of Christian thought on redeemed man: one type that stresses nature and the other that stresses grace—two types of thought which were later to find their heretical exponents in, respectively, Pelagianism and a one-sided predestinationism. But as pre-existence came to the fore, two new types of christology arose which can hardly be considered as intensifications of the two types of Christian anthropology. To a certain extent this might still be said of the christology which emphasizes the divine and in some way or other sacrifices to this the independence of the human element in Jesus (but no longer the reality of his flesh, like Docetism). This is the Alexandrian christology with its Logos-sarx scheme, which has its heretical offshoot in Monophysitism (insofar as this is not merely terminological). But the opposite extreme emphasizes not only the human in Jesus and the independence of this human element, but also accepts with Nicea the pre-existent Logos or Son and thus achieves a duality of operations, natures, subjects, or even persons. This is the Antiochian christology with a scheme of Logos-anthropos, which can be contrasted with the Alexandrian as a duality as opposed to a unity christology; its heretical offshoot is Nestorianism (especially the Nestorianism as conceived by the Alexandrists and later by many Byzantinians).

The Council of Chalcedon brought these christologies together, but did not reconcile them.[3] It wished to honor the contribution of

3. On this most important christological council see the standard work listed by Grillmeier and Bacht in note 1. See also R. V. Sellers, *The Council of Chalcedon. A Historical and Doctrinal Survey,* London, 1961.

both to the Church by pointing out in what way each point was apposite. The unity/unifying christology of Alexandria is valid for the person of Jesus Christ but not for his natures, while the duality christology of Antioch is valid for Christ's natures but not for his person. Thus the pattern of thought arises of the one Christ in two natures, the divine and the human. This pattern absorbs all the divine and all the human that is acknowledged by scripture to Jesus, but adds something unknown to scripture: the distinction of natures. This has become necessary precisely because the pre-existent person was posited and came in Antiochian thought to stand beside the man Jesus. In this situation the Church could not reconcile the element of truth of Antioch with that of Alexandria except by attributing two natures to the one person Jesus Christ. Or, to put it negatively: only in this way could our Christ-confession continue to be maintained for Monophysitism and Nestorianism.

But it was not only with Chalcedon that the pattern of classical christology was born. Chalcedon names the one person of Christ first in a concrete way by indicating it by Jesus' name and titles and by the seven-times repeated "the same," afterwards more technically as the "prosopon" and "hypostasis," in which the divine and the human natures come together (DS 301f.). The latter expression, used also in Pope Leo's letter to Flavian, suggests just as much (or just as little) concerning a pre-existence of the human in Christ as a pre-existence of the divine. The actual personal pre-existence of the Logos or the Son entered the Chalcedonian pattern through later theological expositions, especially that under Alexandrian influence. It is true that the Antiochian contribution in Chalcedon, supported by Leo, still permeated the condemnation of Monoenergism and Monothelitism at the third Council of Constantinople, whose doctrine on the two wills and operations in Christ almost led to the positing of two subjects (DS 556f.). But previously the christology of Alexandrian origin (purged, however, of clear Monophysitism) had proved itself predominant, in the Emperor Zeno's *Henotikon* and in the second Council of Constantinople, which condemned important writings from the Antiochian school.

The unity which emerges in this Alexandrianally oriented christology, especially that of the so-called neo-Chalcedonism,[4] is seen

4. Since a historical and speculative rehabilitation for Antiochian chris-

totally from the viewpoint of the divine Logos. Here the one person in Christ becomes more and more emphatically the divine person. With Leontius of Byzantium the question clearly emerges of how the relation of the hypostasis or person must be expressed for Christ's human nature, and in answer he christologically adapts a definition of hypostasis. For Leontius the human nature of Christ is *enhypostatic,* that is, it exists *in* the divine hypostasis of the Word (*Adv. nestorianos et eutychianos,* I, *passim*). This is an answer that is certainly adopted by every subsequent supporter of Chalcedon, but it gives rise to numerous questions. Particularly in neo-Chalcedonism, Chalcedon appears to be more the beginning than the end.

Questions From the Point of View of This Pattern

The questions which the Chalcedon pattern now begins to raise can be divided into two categories: questions concerning the divine character of Jesus' humanity, or of Jesus in his humanity, and those

---

tology began between the two world wars, many studies now concentrate on the one-sided Alexandrian interpretation of Chalcedon, especially in the Byzantine empire of the sixth century. At that time, side by side and in opposition to one another, there were the following schools: the continuation of Monophysitism (Severus of Antioch), the strict Chalcedonian school (which, however, had its best representatives in the West), and neo-Chalcedonism (especially around the Emperor Justinian). Summaries of the investigations on the latter are given in the articles of Charles Möller, "Le chalcédonisme et le néochalcedonisme en Orient de 451 à la fin du VIe siècle," in Grillmeier and Bacht, *Das Konzil von Chalkedon I,* pp. 637–720; and A. Grillmeier, "Vorbereitung des Mittelalters. Eine Studie über das Verhältnis von Chalkedonismus und Neu-Chalkedonismus in der lateinischen Theologie von Boethius bis zu Gregor dem Grossen," in *ibid.* II, pp. 791–839. Möller defines neo-Chalcedonism as the interpretation of Chalcedon in which the whole of Cyril of Alexandria's ideas (not only his *formula unionis* recognized by Chalcedon, but also his Anathematisms) are accepted and the Antiochians refuted (which was made definite in the condemnation of the "Three Chapters" by Constantinople II, 553). In content this means that Christ has been acknowledged two natures according to Chalcedon but also the formula μία φύσις τοῦ θεοῦ λογοῦ σεσαρκωμένη is maintained, and further the *communicatio idiomatum* ("*unus de Trinitate passus est*") is strongly emphasized. Of most importance is the conviction, ever further elaborated in such neo-Chalcedonism, but also in Chalcedonism, that the person of Christ is divine and *not human.* This is formulated in the enhypostasia and anhypostasia of Christ's humanity by Leontius of Byzantium, who himself was not so much a *neo*-Chalcedonian.

relating to the completeness of his manhood through an individual human person. The question of whether Jesus in his humanity is the natural Son of God rather than adopted son belongs to the first series. It is a question, furthermore, that clearly distinguishes the christological situation after Nicea from that of before, for the natural sonship of the Word is now beyond discussion. During the Carolingian period the question came under discussion in various councils and was answered in the sense of the Alexandrine and neo-Chalcedonian or unity christology: as man, Christ is also God's own, natural Son. With somewhat more difficulty the same answer is later contested against the dialectics of Abelard. Further questions from this former series are concretized on Christ's actions. If Pseudo-Dionysius speaks of "a new divine-human activity" of Christ through which he brings about what is of man in a superhuman way (*Epistola IV; MG* 3, 1072), then here a different accent is detected than that heard when Pope Leo spoke of the actions of both natures (DS 294), and Constantinople III on two actions and two wills (DS 556f). More concrete are the questions whether Jesus has a personally acquired knowledge, whether in his earthly life there was any non-knowing, how far he grew spiritually, and so forth. We shall take up these questions when we consider the being-in-history of Christ on earth.

But now we must review the second series of questions, which is the more important. Has Jesus' human nature also its *own human* personhood or not? Is it enhypostatic in the Word in a way which allows its own hypostasis to exist (and thus causes it to exist), or is it, through being enhypostatic, even *an-hypostatic?* Here too the Alexandrian idea taken up in neo-Chalcedonism was generally the dominant note. Scholasticism, it is true, reaches a certain balance in its full flower: for Thomas, Christ's humanity has its own act of being, which is secondary to the act of being of the Word; for Scotus, personhood is lacking in Christ's humanity only insofar as it is itself a negative definition, but not in its positive aspect. Early and late scholasticism, however, on behalf ·of unity christology, constructed some very strange ontologies. Early scholasticism thought that Christ's humanity may not be logically called a "something" (christological nihilism), or that ontologically it is not a compound of soul and body, but that both individually are assumed in the divine Person of the Word. After the condemnation of such attitudes, deriving from Abelard and his school, the view of the "assumed man" (not "humanity") in Christ enjoyed a certain preference for a time, though curiously enough such theology of *assumptus homo* is sometimes connected with divine predicates of Jesus as man, as with Gerhoch von Reichersberg.[5]

More subtle attempts emerged in late scholasticism to account ontologically for the anhypostasia of Christ's humanity. The most daring, proceeding from a real distinction between essence and act of being, is that of denying a properly created act of being in Christ's humanity and merely have it exist through the divine act of being of the Word itself; others deny Christ's humanity only of a modus—the modus of the *suppositum* of being. The theory of the absence of the individual act of being, which is rightly called the "theory of the ecstasy of being," emerges in Capreolus and took on new life in this century through Louis Billot. This theory perhaps shows up most sharply to what an insoluble problem the Chalcedonian pattern can lead us. On the one hand, it seems to be the logical consequence of Christ's oneness as person: a being that is really one—and a person is considered to be such a being to the highest degree—can have only one act of being. On the other hand, it is precisely the absence of an individually created act of being that makes Christ's human nature completely unreal. Here we come face to face with an ontological Docetism, just as the above mentioned nihilism was a logical Docetism. In contrast to such tendencies is the Scotist assertion that personhood, insofar as it is denied to Christ's humanity, is merely negative—the not-being-assumed—so that eventually nothing of the positive aspects of personhood is absent from this humanity.[6]

A new *assumptus homo* theology, continuing on these lines, has developed since the First World War, led by two French Franciscans, Déodat de Basly and Léon Zeiller. This decisively anti-

5. See L. Ott, "Das Konzil von Chalkedon in der Frühscholastik," in Grillmeier and Bacht, *Das Konzil von Chalkedon II*, pp. 874–922; I. Backes, "Die christologische Problematik der Hochscholastik und ihre Beziehung zu Chalkedon," in *ibid.*, pp. 923–939.

6. A clear survey of the various opinions concerning Christ's human *esse* is given by L. de Raedemaeker: *Metaphysica generalis II*, Louvain, 1935, pp. 426–448.

Alexandrian and particularly anti-Cyrillian christology certainly accepts the doctrine of the Council of Ephesus concerning the one person in Christ, but it no longer functions. Within this person exists the "rational subject" (*sujet intelligent*), and thus an individual ego of the assumed Man Jesus, called "man-God" in deliberate contradiction to the term "God-man." This "man-God" is in constant dialogue or "love-conflict" with God, here not conceived as the Father but as God-Trinity. Pius XII's encyclical *Sempiternus Rex,* on the occasion of the fifteenth centenary of Chalcedon, rejected this ontological dualism within Christ (DS 4905) and heralded the end of this short-lived theory. But only in a first draft of the encyclical, and not in its official published form, a psychological as well as ontological human ego of Jesus is also rejected. The acceptance of such a human "psychological ego" or "act-center" is enjoying more success today, and its most eminent advocate is Galtier.[7]

Objections to the Chalcedonian Pattern

When we began this exposition on patterns of thought, we also mentioned their dangers. This has already been demonstrated for the Chalcedonian pattern. But further criticism of this pattern is not only possible, it is indeed necessary. Yet it must be affirmed that even the biblical christology patterns are merely patterns. This is already obvious from their multiplicity and their origin in history. Furthermore, the biblical patterns today cannot simply be assumed. Patterns such as that of "the Messiah" and "the Lord" ask for translation, and "the Servant of Yahweh" for further reflection, insofar as it concerns, for example, vicarious suffering. Perhaps such further thinking on New Testament christology will lead us to connect the patterns, for example by understanding the Lordship of the risen Christ as his sealed and eternalized servanthood. Such biblical christologies, moreover, sooner or later have to confront the pattern originating from Chalcedon. The task we have set ourselves, however, points in the opposite direction. Here we shall offer an explanation of ecclesiastical christology, and thus an elaboration on the Chalce-

7. See A. Grillmeier's study in J. Feiner, J. Trütsch, F. Böckle, *Theology Today,* London, 1965.

donian pattern. That broad use will be made of biblical christology is obvious from the foregoing. It will become clearer still if we now discuss the objections which can be listed against the Chalcedonian pattern. The most important, the doubts concerning Christ's humanity, have already been mentioned. We shall, however, list other objections which have emerged especially in Reformation theology.

First of all, an objection can be raised against the application of the concept of "nature" in general. This objection is primarily valid within modern usage, which places "nature" in opposition to and beneath the person and his self-expression: culture. The term φύσις used in patristic times did not yet have this limitation and simply expressed the reality of a determined being. It was a matter in Chalcedon of the whole reality which answers to the divine and human being. Within the text of Chalcedon itself we find another concept which helps us to define the "nature" concept more closely, namely, that of the equality of substance or unity of substance. Nicea had declared that the Son is of one substance, ὁμοούσιος, with the Father; Chalcedon amplifies this by saying that Christ is of one substance with the Father as regards his Godhead and at the same time of one substance with us as regards his manhood. This gives us the right, in this christological context, to understand φύσις and οὐσία as synonyms. Divine and human nature quite simply indicate everything pertaining respectively to the divine and the human, by which Jesus Christ is one in being respectively with the Father and with us.

But then there is a second objection, that here the divine and the human arise in equal relation and are grouped together under the expression "two" natures. If this were really to mean that the nature- or substance-concept is applied equally to the divine and the human in Christ, then the two-nature pattern would indeed lead us to gross errors. For those who formulated the Chalcedonian dogma, it was a matter in this text not of the relation between God and creature in itself, but only of the presence of all the divine and all the human in the one Christ. They acknowledge the incommensurability of the divine and the human as, for example, Nicea did, but they did not elaborate their relation in Christ himself. Later theologians have pointed out the totally analogous way according to which the concept of "nature" is used both times in Christ; the fact that divine and human nature do not merge as parts to form one great whole, since the divine cannot be inserted into a greater whole; the fact also that the number "two" does not then have the proper function of numbers, namely, to indicate the multiplicity of like quantities. Yet it remains a task for those who proceed from the two-nature pattern, to reflect constantly on the dissimilarity of these "two." If the idea had always prevailed that because of this dissimilarity the divine and the human never appear in a competitive relationship, then the theories on the anhypostasia of Christ's humanity as the real absence of a created perfection would never have arisen.

If we think further on the two natures, then the fact that this concept does not make christology physical, but essentialistic, can rate as a third objection. If the nature or essence of Christ is under discussion, then for many modern men this is no longer concerned with our existence, and it represents Christ to us merely as an object of knowledge. Such a view detaches christology from soteriology. This objection holds for many christological treatises which, as formal elaborations of the *unio hypostatica,* are completely distinct from soteriology. The objection holds even more for the dogmatic formula of Chalcedon itself, but then only insofar as this is detached from its context within and without this council. The creed of Nicea-Constantinople also belongs to this context with the "because of us men and because of our salvation" as Christ's motive for becoming man; as well as the letters of Cyril and Leo which were accepted by Chalcedon; and finally the whole of patristic literature, which on the one hand preaches Christ's divinity because we would otherwise not become one with God, and on the other hand accepts his complete humanity because otherwise not all of our human existence would be redeemed. This entails that for Greek thought the very assumption of human nature by the Word does not mean only or even primarily the acceptance of Jesus' individual human existence, but of the nature which is common to him and us. Thus the acceptance of human nature for Greek thought already includes redemption, and our general christological treatises would through this concept alone take on more life. Yet the pattern of Chalcedon demands amplification through an elaboration of how the redemption which is inherent in the divine and human natures of Christ comes to us via the paths of human communication. The assumption

63

of our nature is concretely the communion of Jesus with us in word, deed, and attitude, in suffering and dying and as resurrected. For that reason the two-nature pattern must be filled with biblical categories such as that of "Lord" and "Servant" and our categories of intersubjectivity.

A fourth objection is intimately related to this problem. The Chalcedonian pattern says nothing on Jesus' place in the history of salvation, which is precisely what the biblical patterns, insofar as they are "messianic," certainly do. This confronts us with the task of also making the transcendence of Christ through his divine nature visible in the history of salvation, by illustrating his eschatological meaning.

A fifth deficiency in the two-nature pattern is that it does not show us Jesus' own history of salvation or at least not the sequence of the salvific phases within his divine-human existence. In the books of the New Testament all the divine and all the human that is expressed by the confession of the two natures of Jesus is equally confessed of him and only the distinction regarding the "non-mingling" of the natures, so emphasized by Chalcedon, is lacking. In its place is the distinction between Jesus' earthly and glorified life, which is precisely what is lacking in the Chalcedonian model. The keenest expression of this distinction is found in the christological hymn of Philippians 2, 6–11, but in some form or other it turns up again and again—as, for example, already in the difference between subject and predicate of the New Testament's most concise confession: "Jesus is Lord." Here too it will be our task to fill in the two-nature schema, in itself empty, as far as possible with Jesus' history and certainly to elaborate it for Jesus' earthly and glorified life. Is the proportion between the divine and the human in Christ perhaps not the same during these two phases of his existence?

Finally, for the sixth objection there are the various problems which have arisen in consequence of the Chalcedonian pattern of thought. What precisely can be stated concerning the *divine* sonship of Jesus as *man:* is he *as man* the son or the adopted son of God? And especially: what can we say about the enhypostasia and the anhypostasia of this individual human nature? Is Jesus' human personality absorbed in that of the Word, and if so is he then depersonalized as man? Or does it exist as an individual human center of acts, decisions, and self-consciousness beside the divine person of the Word and in competition with it? To take this aporia to its apex we could ask: does the Chalcedonian pattern lead us to a disguised or to a divided Christ?

This long critical review of the most current pattern of christology shows us clearly to which questions we must seek an answer. First and foremost there is the question of anhypostasia. Related to this are questions on the divinized and soteriological character of Christ's humanity, his uniqueness in relation to God and to mankind. Thereby the question of the *unio hypostatica,* the redemptive significance of Christ, comes to the fore. Thus an attempt can be made to meet the first, second, third, fifth, and sixth objections. Only the elaboration of the Chalcedonian pattern for the phases of Christ's individual existence is outside the scheme, but it has been elaborated at such length and so circumstantially by theology in an a-historical manner that we can best begin a correction of it by abstracting Jesus' history. It will be obvious, however, that such a correction leads us to Christ's place in our history of salvation and thus also to his own history, the history of his earthly humiliation and his heavenly glory, for only as the Glorified does he fully assume a place in our history. Our subsequent exposition can then be divided into two main parts: a more atemporal view *of the man who is God's Son,* and after that the human history of this Son of God, *the earthly and glorified existence of Christ.*

So we hope to complement and correct the current christological pattern. The result will perhaps be less "mythical" or "religious" and more human. Certainly Christ may not be confessed as less divine than the Church has confessed him, especially in Chalcedon. It is striking that the "quest for the historical Jesus" of the nineteenth century and of our times, after having discarded the dogma and also the kerygma concerning Christ, eventually salvaged a Jesus broadly coinciding with the researcher himself: a liberal Jesus, a social reformer, a free existence, a high point of evolution.[8] This is heartening, for it shows how much God's Son is "consubstantial

---

8. H. Berkhof, "Christologie en Christus-prediking in verband met de huidige beleving der werkelijkheid," *Nederl. Theol. Tijdschrift* 21 (1967), 370–386.

with us." But the plurality and one-sidedness of the different out-looks also confront us with the question of in how far we bring Jesus Christ himself into the discussion, of in how far we give an answer to his question: "Whom do you say that *I* am?" We write what follows, then, in the hope that the Spirit who leads us along the path of these thought patterns may keep us on that path which leads to the full truth and the whole Christ, that he may remind us of everything that Jesus has said and what he was and is for us.

1. THE MAN WHO IS GOD'S SON

It is always desirable in discussion to use what is most certain as the point of departure, although everyone is not always agreed on what is most certain. In our case, however, certainly one point can be accepted by all, and for that reason can be called the most certain. It is the fact that Jesus Christ is one person, a fact so self-evident for most people that it is often ignored. First we will define this oneness of his person and draw some formal conclusions. Afterwards we can then discuss the two natures of Christ. Here the best point of departure for us as men is the humanity of Jesus—and that again is a self-evident presupposition of all christology, especially biblical christology. After that we shall take up the divine sonship, and then finally return again to the one person of Jesus Christ, now to examine his human transcendence, which places him in our history of salvation. That will lead us to the second part, regarding Jesus' own salvific history.

The One Person Jesus Christ

He whose proper name is Jesus of Nazareth and whose title of "Messiah" in the Greek translation of "Christ" has become a second proper name, Jesus Christ, is one person. This fact, as we have said, is universally accepted. In the books of the New Testament it is a supposition no one reflects on: everyone knows who is being spoken of when the names "Jesus" or "Christ" are pronounced. The concept of "person" does not itself appear in the New Testament, in christology just as little as in theology. It only comes to function in

christology when Christ's oneness becomes problematical. This occurred in Antiochian theology, and even there only after the individual nature of the man Jesus was posited beside the consubstan-
tiality of the Son with the Father as pronounced by Nicea. Since
then a theme of Antiochian christology is the distinction, the duality
even, of the divine and the human in Christ. But a duality of natures
or of persons? This question, based on modern terminology, cannot
be answered unequivocally, as we are concerned here with authors
who had still not made our distinction between nature and person.
It is certainly probable that the Antiochians in general, and also
Nestorius—in contrast to the idea that Cyril of Alexandria had of
him—did not accept a clean-cut duality of persons in Christ, however difficult it was for them to see everywhere the unity of the
divine and human in Jesus, especially in his suffering. We can trace
this tendency of the Antiochian school in all christologies which,
after Nicea, wish to emphasize the human element in Jesus. A
duality is posited by Leo I and by Chalcedon. It threatens to become
a duality of persons in the later *assumptus-homo* theologies,
especially in the school of Déodat de Basly. But even if a human
"ego" in Christ is discussed less ontologically and more psychologically, the personal oneness of Christ becomes problematical. For so
far as modern man continues to hold with the Nicene creed, this
oneness must be problematical, for we are today, just as much as
the Antiochians (and scripture itself), convinced of the genuine
manhood of Jesus. In fact, we are even more compelled than the
Antiochians to credit a duality of persons in Christ in that our
attention is claimed not only by the completeness of the human
nature in Christ, but first and foremost by his individual history and
its inherent personal decisions.

In contrast, the personal oneness of Jesus Christ remains the
primary factor, not only in Scripture and for those who still find no
problems in it, but also in the disputes themselves. The Alexandrians
are correct in assuming the personal oneness, and already for that
reason alone have a right to more esteem than they enjoy today. But
further, all of the Antiochian tendencies have retained, or have tried
to retain in one way or another, the personal oneness in their image
of Christ. Where Leo and the third Council of Constantinople wish
to speak of two *formae* or two wills in the actions of Christ as

though they were two subjects, nevertheless in the one person is expressly named. In the Council of Chalcedon's own contribution, it is true that the duality of natures is the most individual expression, but the oneness of the person receives at least as much emphasis. For before the terms "nature" and "person" are introduced, Christ's divine and human characteristics are acknowledged to someone who is called "the same" seven times (DS 301), and after the two natures are distinguished it is said that these fuse in one πρόσωπον and one ὑπόστασις (DS 302), which terms can be translated as: in one not merely nominal but also real person. Even the less well-balanced Antiochian-inspired trends did not abandon the one person in Christ. In the school of Déodat de Basly one comes closest to it, but the pronouncement of Chalcedon remains too explicit to be contradicted on this point.

For that reason the personal oneness in Christ, or more accurately the oneness of the person Jesus Christ, is the point of departure for our christological examination. We can now pass on to the following section, for the concept of "one person," at least formally, needs no further explanation. Yet even very simple theories can be clarified and further consolidated by considering what points conflict or can possibly come into conflict. This we shall now do summarily.

1. What are most in conflict with Christ's one person are those expressions which suggest that there is within him, within his being, a covenant, or a dialogue, or even a polarity. Déodat de Basly is certainly one of those who go farthest in this regard: the "man-God" is involved in a love-conflict with "God-Trinity" and therefore apparently also with God the Son. Less explicit than this systematically developed idea are the scattered expressions found in all kinds of writers in which Christ is described according to each of the two natures as respectively the High Priest who brings the sacrifice and the Son who, with the Father and in the same way as the Father, accepts this same sacrifice, as the man who worships and as God who is worshipped. Of course, in scripture Jesus Christ is the one who comes to us from God and at the same time the one who prays to God his Father, who sacrifices before Him. But nothing indicates that this would divide his person. That Christ receives our

prayer and sacrifice with the Father is not a scriptural factor, and much less still the fact that he would do this in the same way as the Father. Thus scripture teaches us nothing of a moral or virtual dual personality in Christ which would divide his person, it tells us only of a mediatorship in which we can distinguish two directions— which, however, are scarcely to be distinguished explicitly in scripture itself.[9] In place of this the New Testament shows us, especially in the gospels, Jesus' dialogue with the Father. Not a divine Son, but the heavenly Father, is the thou of the man Jesus. For so far as something of Jesus' inner life shines through in the gospels, it is not primarily the self-expression of an I but the being fulfilled with the Thou of the Father. In the synoptic gospels the main theme of Jesus' preaching is the Father's kingdom, and his self-revelation merely contributes to bringing this kingdom about. When for John this self-revelation becomes the main theme, it always occurs in connection with statements on the Father: the Johannine Jesus also expresses his I only from and to the Father. This dialogue between Father and Son can guard us against assuming a dialogue within Jesus himself. Moreover, carried to its logical conclusion, such a dialogue divides Jesus' person at least psychologically and such a division would in a normal psyche also indicate an ontological duality in the person as such.

2. The same is also but to a lesser degree the case if one posits an individual subject on the side of Christ's humanity. As we have already noted, Pope Pius XII, in his encyclical *Sempiternus Rex,* rejected the assumption of an ontological human subject beside the person of the Word, but not the assumption of a *psychological* human subject or ego. This opinion may not be regarded as heretical. We can learn much from it, as will become clear in the following. For the moment, however, it should be pointed out that at least it does not consistently express the oneness of Christ's person. If Christ's oneness is that of an ontological person, the man

9. A certain schematization of the two directions is to be found in the "christology of call and response" elaborated by Paul M. van Buren in his book *The Secular Meaning of the Gospel,* New York, 1963 (in which the passage on this subject seems to be rather ill located; see the author's remark on p. 18); and by Dietrich Ritschl in *Memory and Hope,* New York, 1967, esp. pp. 213–224.

Jesus being therein a psychological person, subject, or ego, or even an individual act-center, then it can at least be said that such a difference is not presented to us in Scripture. It also makes Christ less understandable, unless precisely the ontological person is done away with, which again is done with a bad conscience unless one wants to deny him. If one investigates the distinction made in these ideas more profoundly, then it does not seem to hold. What in fact is an ontological person who does not exist in consciousness and freedom even psychologically as an ego and act-center? And conversely: is a psychological act-center or consciousness completely an ego or a self-consciousness if the ontological person who bears it is not constantly consciously present in it, certainly as co-conscious, but also thus defining the whole content of consciousness? If in Jesus Christ the human ego or act-center stands psychologically outside his ontological person, it is then clearly not the ego or act-center of Jesus. And if therein the ontological person of Christ is not itself conscious and does not speak to us, then Jesus as man is in this regard not different from us and the Christ or the Son has disappeared behind the man Jesus without being of significance for our salvation. But let it be said again that we shall later be learning much from the theologians now being criticized. Then we shall perhaps express more radically what they regard as essential, but in order to do so we must first point out their contradictions.

3. What is introduced in modern theology in the duality of subjects has long been present where divine and human operations were distinguished, but without special reflection on their concurrence. When Leo says that "each nature (*forma*) has its own operation," he adds in the same sentence: "in common with the other one." The decree of Constantinople III against the Monothelites repeats this whole formula and adds to the distinction of operations that they are never in conflict with one another and that the human will is subjected to the divine will. Yet within the Chalcedonian pattern this concurrence of operations has not always had the attention it deserved. While in modern christology, as we have just pointed out, the human operation was given a proper existence "over against" the Logos,[10] long before, the current discussion on the

10. Together with other theologians Karl Rahner thinks he must conclude this "over against" from the condemnation of Monotheletism. In

God-man had in due course completely freed the divine operations from the human. Especially in rhetorical expressions, the majesty of the creative act as God was measured out broadly against his human indigence. In the Christmas hymn *Altitudo quid hic jaces,* he who lights the torches of heaven suffers from the cold; while in the hymn *A solis ortus cardine,* he who feeds the birds is fed with mother's milk. It is remarkable that in scripture the first is ascribed not to the Son but to the Father. An individual operation of the Son in his divinity, apart from his human existence, is not even clearly indicated in the pre-existence texts. We shall therefore also have to be careful on the side of the divinity with the acceptance of a separate act-center. We shall return to this question later; here it is sufficient to have established the oneness of Christ's person as the point of departure.

The Completeness of Christ's Manhood

That Jesus is a man is just as much a presupposition of the New Testament as the fact that he is one person. But even in the books of the New Testament this manhood is expressly brought into the foreground, especially where it contrasts with the divine dignity which is inherent in Christ from the beginning (Philippians 2, 7; John 1, 1–14), or where it expresses itself in the fact that Jesus undergoes temptation and suffering (Hebrews 2, 9; 4, 15). In the Hellenistic world this suffering is the pre-eminent sign of Christ's manhood and of his equality with us. Long before Chalcedon named Christ equal with us in substance, ὁμοούσιος ἡμῖν, Justin designated Him as equal with us in suffering, ὁμοιοπαθής ἡμῖν (*Dial. c. Tryph.* 48, 3). For Nestorius it is precisely the suffering which is the point

---

"Current Problems in Christology" (in *Theological Investigations I*, Baltimore and Dublin, 1963, pp. 149–200) he says on p. 157f., "Now it may and indeed must be said that the doctrine of the unconfused and unchanged real human nature implies, as the struggle against Monotheletism after the rejection of monophysitism shows, that the 'human nature' of the Logos possesses a genuine, spontaneous, free, spiritual, active center, a human self-consciousness, which creaturely faces the eternal Word in a genuinely human attitude of adoration, obedience, a most radical sense of creaturehood." The words "creaturely faces the eternal Word" translate the German *"dem ewigen Wort kreatürlich gegenüberstehe,"* in which the "over against" (gegenüber) occurs.

on which he is inclined to see two subjects in Christ. Pope Leo uses the suffering and the death of Jesus to contrast his human *forma* with the divine: "He could die by virtue of the one and he could not die by virtue of the other. . . . The one radiates through miracles, the other undergoes hatred" (DS 294). Yet Christ's manhood is not limited to suffering, it comprises all of our existence except sin, thus also positive realities as well as the spiritual soul of man. The saying "what is not assumed (by the Word), is not made whole (or redeemed)" is used first of all against Apollinaris to defend the existence of such a spiritual soul in Christ. The "one in substance with us" of Chalcedon forms a distinct parallel with the "one in substance with the Father" adopted by Nicea. Christ is by nature (φύσις) or substance (οὐσία) similar to every man.

These two concepts of Chalcedon serve to render the whole scriptural and traditional confession of Christ's manhood and its salvific meaning. They must then be interpreted in the light of this point of departure, and not vice versa. "Nature" and "substance" cannot thus be applied in a sense which was unknown to those who used these terms in Chalcedon or at least was not then intended by them. For that reason, and this is self-evident, the term "nature" should not be interpreted here from the modern contradistinction between "nature" and "person." The question of whether Christ is a human person is thus not decided in a negative way by saying that Chalcedon acknowledged to him merely a human nature; the answer will have to be sought from the point of departure itself of this confession. The same obtains for the scholastic distinction between essence and act of being (*essentia* and *esse*), especially when Thomism sees this distinction as not merely emanating from our rational thinking (*distinctio rationis*), but as independent of it, given in the created reality (*distinctio realis*). Here again the question of whether Christ has an individual human and thus created act of being—a question which, as we said, was intensively discussed in late scholasticism—cannot be decided negatively by saying that Chalcedon merely acknowledged a human essence in Christ; again the answer will have to be sought from the whole of scripture and tradition. Just as the concepts of "nature" and "essence" do not exclude person or act of being, so do they not exclude growth and historicity. The only thing that is *not* implied in the general terms used by Chalcedon are the individual characteristics. For that reason the saying "what is not assumed is not redeemed" may be understood only of the specific nature and not of these characteristics. In other words, Christ would not have to be a woman, an atomic physicist, or a Japanese in order to be redeemer for women, atomic physicists, and Japanese. We are thus constantly referred to the whole picture of scripture and tradition in order to give Christ's manhood a more detailed content.

In this light human personhood, and thus an individual human-being and -becoming, and a human position in history, not only may not be excluded, but must be positively awarded to Jesus Christ. Further on, Christ's individuality and historicity will be discussed, but here we are concerned with his humanity and personhood. These must unhesitatingly be awarded to Christ. For what does it mean if one denies in him a human, created act of being? Then Jesus Christ is no longer a man, then he *is* no longer as a man. Christ would be more mutilated in this view than through Apollinarianism, for not only has what makes him a rational being been taken away, but also what simply makes him a being in the world. Something similar can be said of all those theories which make Christ's human nature anhypostatic by denying human personhood in Christ, at least insofar as this is intended as a positive perfection. Then Jesus Christ is again not a man, for what is a man who is not a person, does not have control as person of his own attitude, his own fate, his own being, by his decisions? The Jesus who prays to the Father and is tempted like us is being denied here. In such a case the saying "what is not assumed is not healed, not redeemed" is certainly apt. We might now add to that: is not healing, is not redeeming.

The appeal to the reality of Jesus Christ as man can be strengthened still more by the idea that God when he communicates himself does not exclude the operations and perfections of being of his creatures, but on the contrary includes them as much as possible. However, God in his creation does not work merely from outside, he is at the same time immanent in it and works from within, and this means that he acts in union with his creatures. We can also say that God's activity and self-communication perfects his creatures and does not deprive them, so that we can expect the loss of a perfection only for the sake of another creature, not for the sake of God himself. Or from the point of view of the creatures: they participate as much as possible in God also through working and communicating themselves, and will thus thereby attain perfections instead of losing them. All of these reasons tell against the loss of individual personhood and still more of an individual act of being in Christ. They even tell against this loss if one says that the person and the act of being of the Word supplement this loss in an eminent way. For can one seriously speak of a supplementation if precisely in the human, created reality the being and the being-person are lacking? Neither in this theory can one refer to the mystery of the redemption through the cross and death and thus include these, as it were, already in the structure of Jesus' person. Rather than intensifying the mystery of the cross, all of these theories appear to be a denial of it, for they deprive the man who undergoes death on the cross his human reality and thus the reality of Jesus' suffering and death itself. From the relation between God and creature everything therefore tells against the denial of Christ's individual human personhood and own human being. Moreover, from the point of view of the God-creature relation everything tells in favor of the acceptance of such human personhood.

This latter formula is important because it is positive. That God's operations and self-communication in Christ demand precisely a human personhood continues to hold if we now look more closely at the motive of the ideas that we have been discussing. Their advocates do not say that an individual personhood or an individual act of being is absent in the man Jesus because of his union with God in general, but specifically because he is united with God the Son in one person. One person cannot bear in himself a human personhood beside the divine, one person cannot have two acts of being. This is true, but this does not render the arguments in favor of a proper human personhood invalid. For that reason we shall have to find an answer to the argument taken from the divine person. Thus we arrive at our third consideration.

Christ's Divine Sonship

Jesus Christ is one person. He is a human person. Can he then still be called a divine person? He is so called in the Chalcedonian pattern, but not precisely in the individual formula of Chalcedon itself—only by those who prepared and elaborated Chalcedon. We have already pointed out that the pre-existence of the Logos or the Son was conceived ever more clearly as a personal existence and that this to a certain extent found its culmination in Nicea. Cyril and the Alexandrian theologians speak of the Word that assumes flesh (and not merely becomes flesh). Pope Leo also proceeds from this concept: "The Son of God appears within these lowest spheres[11] of the universe, descending from his heavenly seat and not swerving from the Father's glory . . . for invisible in his own he has become visible in us." In Chalcedon itself, on the other hand, the one person of Christ is not described on or from the basis of his pre-existence, but is much more the result of a concurrence of the natures. Shortly after this, however, especially in neo-Chalcedonism, the Alexandrian influence became stronger, and since then, as we have already seen, both the problems of the theologians and the unreflected expressions of faith on Christ have been controlled by the pre-existent divine person. Jesus Christ is a divine person, for he is personally the same as the eternal Son of the Father, the Second Person of the Most Holy Trinity. What must we do with this affirmation, what can we do with it, now that the one person Jesus Christ would already seem to be a human person? We shall first sketch a few other answers in order to come to our own suggestion.

NO PROBLEM?

A first answer could consist in denying the problem itself. The divine and the human do not stand as homogeneous objects beside one another and thus cannot be added to one another. One does not then have to suppose two persons when one assumes in Christ a divine and a human person. This answer fits completely in the line of our study *God or man: a false dilemma;* for our case, however, it is not conclusive. First of all, it demonstrates too much. Neither can one, by reason of the same "non-numerability," speak of one person in Christ: numerals cannot really be employed when bringing the divine into contact with the human. Moreover, the question

11. DS 294. We translate here the reading *"haec mundi infima"* in place of the *"infirma"* of the Denziger edition.

remains of whether regarding such contact the word "one" can rightly be used, however metaphorically, as long as a divine and a human person in Christ are admitted. Then the dialogue which is carried out between God and man (again analogously with the dialogue between men) would have to be placed within Christ himself, whereas it was argued above that in such a case the primary factor of his one person and the dialogue described in the gospels of Jesus with the Father are being denied, or at least obscured. For that reason, the non-numerability of the divine and the human in itself does not make it possible to place a divine person in Christ beside the human and yet to say that he is one person. We shall have to investigate the divine in Christ more closely.

KENOTIC THEORIES

The kenotic theories can be regarded as a second answer to the problem. In the Lutheranism of the sixteenth and seventeenth centuries Luther's care for the unity of Christ and on the other hand for his actually having flesh aroused great interest in the "emptying" of him who existed in divine form as mentioned in Philippians 2, 7. This theme, elaborated in particular by Chemnitz, is fortunately again attracting interest in Catholic christology.[12] Here we must turn our attention to the revival of kenosis christology in the nineteenth century. In old Lutheranism it was described how the Son of God who had already become man rid himself in his human nature of those divine characteristics which by virtue of the exchange of idioms given with the *unio hypostatica* (*communicatio idiomatum*) are due to this *human* nature itself. In the nineteenth century, however, it was a matter of an emptying which the Logos itself accomplishes in its divine nature through becoming man. He empties himself of divine attributes which are due to this *divine* nature. According to the most important supporter of this theory, Thomasius, the Son did retain the absolute divine attributes,

---

12. A historical survey of the Reformation kenosis theories is given by W. Pannenberg, *Jesus—God and Man*, Philadelphia, 1967, pp. 307–323. For an interpretation of Philippians 2, 7 see P. Schoonenberg, "He Emptied Himself," in *Who Is Jesus of Nazareth?* (*Concilium*, vol. 11), New York, 1965, pp. 47–66.

which are due to God apart from his relation to the world, but he eradicated the relative attributes, referring to the world, such as omnipotence, omniscience, and omnipresence. Precisely in emptying himself of the latter attributes, the first, the inalienable divine attributes, such as freedom and love, come to expression. The divine self-consciousness of the Son is here limited to a growing self-consciousness such as is peculiar to men. This idea of a divine kenosis found supporters in Russian orthodoxy and Anglicanism, and elements of it can be found among others.

The idea has something biblical about it and today it has a special appeal. Perhaps its most eminent merit lies in the fact that it shows us God in Jesus as stripped of those attributes, not which God had to lay aside, but which *we* wholly or partly falsely have acknowledged to God. It has also rightly made the idea of God's immutability capable of greater nuance. Yet it must also be criticized on this very point. For does it attribute to the Son in his divine nature a divine mutability, or actually only a human one? Can God become poor when he enriches us in the incarnation of the Son? Perhaps supporters of the kenosis theory can retort that the divine emptying is provisional and becomes in Jesus' glorification a divine self-communication of God. But then the dispute would have to be shifted to the relation between emptying and glorification in Christ. At the moment only the question of whether this theory has succeeded in presenting Jesus Christ with his human person and his divinity as one person is important. At first sight, this would seem to be the case, for such a doctrine of the divine kenosis is at bottom an inverted Monophysitism and an inverted Alexandrian christology. As in Monophysitism humanity would be absorbed in the glory of the Godhead, so here the godhead threatens to be absorbed, or even to be submerged in, the lowliness of the humanity. But on one point the comparison is defective and precisely here the kenosis theory seems unable to solve the problem of Christ's single personality. The Alexandrians and all those who think along such lines sacrifice Christ's human *person* to the divine person, but the kenoticists refuse to do the reverse. The Logos or the Son remains the divine person who rids himself in freedom from his relative attributes, so that there is during the emptying still a divine person. We can even say that the kenoticists themselves ultimately think according to the Alexandrian pattern, for the person who is limited in his being-man remains divine. For them Jesus does not become a human person. Moreover, there is still one point on which their theory can prove of no service: even if they were to solve the problem of the single personality for Christ's earthly life, this solution becomes irrelevant when the earthly life ends and the emptying changes into glory. And it is precisely thus that Christ now stands before us.

THE THOMIST DOCTRINE OF THE TRINITY

We cannot place the person of the Son beside the man Jesus in such a way that there is a dialogue within himself. We must then reflect more closely on this divine person. The theory of a divine self-emptying falls short precisely on this point. But we have not far to look for it. For a third answer lies in the concepts of the fathers and the scholastics regarding the divine persons. These Three were at first distinguished only by name, as occurs in the symbols of baptism. If there was a technical term arises, it was primarily ὑπόστασις, which means "reality standing by itself," "substance," and for that reason is rendered in Latin by "*substantia*," and later in technical language made more emphatic by "*suppositum*." The Greek word πρόσωπον, which originally meant "mask" and "role," still continues for Greek ears to indicate less an independent being than "*persona*" for Latins, although this word had the same original meanings. If *persona* becomes in Western theology the actual substitute of the Greek ὑπόστασις, it nevertheless does not coincide, certainly in the doctrine on the Trinity, with our modern concept of person, where consciousness and freedom are in the forefront. The concept of person which passed on from patristic to scholastic theology, however, was laid down in Boethius's well-known definition: *individua substantia rationalis naturae,* the individual substance of a rational nature. Thomas Aquinas uses this definition in his doctrine on the Trinity and also names that of Richard of St. Victor: *rationalis naturae incommunicabilis existentia,* the inalienable existence of a rational nature.[13] In the elaboration of these

13. Boethius, *Tractatus V* (opusculum contra Eutychen et Nestorium), c. 5; Richardus a. S. Victore, *De trinitate IV,* 18 and 23; St. Thomas, *Summa theol.* I, q. 29, a. 1 and a. 3 and 4.

definitions the emphasis is on the moment of the existing in itself (and not in something else), on the *individua substantia* or *incommunicabilis existentia*. The rational nature in which the person exists certainly distinguishes it from the other *supposita,* but it is only added to the existing-in-itself from outside. The idea that consciousness and freedom are precisely the highest forms of the existing-in-itself plays no part in scholastic doctrine on the Trinity. More precisely, consciousness and freedom are for Thomas and in Thomism deliberately eliminated from the Trinitarian concept of person. The divine persons have no individual consciousness and freedom, but realize in a relative way the consciousness and freedom common to all three. Schillebeeckx has clearly described this Thomist concept in its christological consequence by saying that the Son is conscious of his sonship not in a divine but only in his human consciousness.[14]

This is not the place to discuss the Thomist theory directly in its value as doctrine of the Trinity. Christologically, however, it is of very great merit, for it is a step towards the solution of the problem. We can see that Thomas did not need to struggle with personal unity and that in passing he even names the human nature of Christ itself as the person of the Word.[15] For if the Son indeed has no individual consciousness and freedom as divine person, while Jesus certainly does have it as human person, then there are certainly not two subjects within Christ which are person in the same way, thus no concurrence of two conscious freedoms, thus no dialogue. Yet the question is whether the Thomist solution is consistent enough. It excludes a psychological dual personality in Christ, but does it also exclude an ontological dual personality? The difficulty still remains that the human person in Christ has a divine person beside itself, while this Christ is one person. It is then worthwhile to search further in the direction indicated, for example by

14. E. Schillebeeckx, "Het bewustzijnsleven van Christus," in *Tijdschrift voor Theologie I* (1961), 227–251; see p. 241.

15. *Summa theol.* III, q. 2, a. 10c: "*humana natura assumpta est ad hoc quod sit persona Filii Dei.*" Thus the written tradition against the correction of the ed. Leonina: "*quod sit personae*" and the Marietti edition: "*quod sit in persona.*" See E. Schillebeeckx, "Persoonlijke openbaringsgestalte van de Vader," in *Tijdschrift voor Theologie* 6 (1966), 274–288, p. 278, note 5.

asking what the discussion on the divine person of the Son means in connection with the whole Christian message of salvation.

HERMENEUTICS OF THE PRE-EXISTENCE TEXTS

The fourth answer, which in our opinion is conclusive, consists in the fact that we put the theological and the magisterial discussion on the Son as divine, transcendent, and pre-existent person back in the context it originally had and thus interpret it according to what it meant in that context. It is worthwhile pointing out that this procedure is necessary wherever the past speaks to us, that it is necessary precisely in order to understand theological statements, that it is no less important with regard to dogma. Especially is the christological dogma a handing on of the confession of Jesus' unique and definitive salvific meaning. Jesus is God's ultimate and complete word, God's act of redemption for us, and thus God is redemptively present in him and for us in a way which surpasses all God's previous salvific actions, and this forms a definitive beginning in human history. This is true not only for the glorified Christ, it is also true for Jesus in his earthly life, and it is also true for his origin. It is on the basis of this idea that we have approached the pre-existence of Word or Son. *Consequently, everything that is said about his divinity in his pre-existence is done in connection with Jesus Christ, and nothing is said outside this connection.*

This is most clear in the New Testament, which presents either a predestination of us and Christ before the creation (Romans 8, 29; see Ephesians 1, 9–11) or the orientation of everything to him (Colossians 1, 15–17), or God's operation culminating in himself. Personal pre-existence emerges most strongly where Christ is sent into the world or comes from the Father (Galatians 4, 4; Hebrews 10, 5; 1 Timothy 3, 16; John 3, 13, 31; 6, 62; 16, 28; 1 John 4, 2; 2 John 7), or where he was already with the Father in the beginning John 1, 1) and possessed his glory there before the creation (John 17, 5). But all these words wish to express what Jesus Christ is now and what he now means for us. To limit ourselves to the two last texts quoted: the whole prologue wishes to express who is the Jesus of St. John's gospel, and Jesus names his glory before the world was made in order to receive it now from the Father.

This plan does not essentially alter with tradition. It could become different only if tradition were able to invoke data other than the biblical preaching of Christ, which cannot be proved. On the other hand, it can certainly be demonstrated that the bond with the concrete Jesus Christ is never lost in the discussion on pre-existence. For Justin, the Logos is not primarily described in his relation to the Father, but as imparted to heathen philosophers and showing himself in the Old Testament theophanies before he appears wholly in Jesus Christ. Justin occasionally thinks of the Logos as a power of God, but personalizes him precisely in his mission as "angel or "apostle" into the world. If the Logos concept is later no longer so clearly related to the world, nevertheless the Son concept is occasionally related to the incarnation, as for example in Hippolytus. And even if the names "Logos" and "Son" no longer spontaneously refer to the world, they still continue to function in a context of Jesus Christ and his salvific operations. This is certainly obscured by speculations proceeding from God's eternity (the Father is eternally Father and must thus eternally have a Son), or by Origen's Platonic tendency to consider all the spiritual (not merely the Logos but also the souls) as pre-existent with regard to the material world and its history. But Origen's concept is also a prologue to the gospel of redemption through the Christ born of Mary. If the Council of Nicea describes the only-begotten Son as of one substance with the Father before mentioning his becoming flesh, and if Constantinople I renders this birth from the substance of the Father as a birth "before all ages," then it may not be forgotten that the words "God's only-begotten Son" and what follows are in apposition to the "one Lord Jesus Christ," a name which already presupposes his incarnation. How little the magisterial discussions of the Church were concerned with the pre-existence itself of the Son would appear obvious from the fact that Pope Leo and the Council of Chalcedon spoke of the concurrence of Godhead and humanity in one person. This expression implies just as much a pre-existence of the human nature as of the Son; neither did the councils criticize the "from two natures" of the Monophysites; they only added to it the "in two natures." Consequently, where Leo and Chalcedon spoke of a "coming together in one person," this one person of Christ is to be called divine-human rather than merely divine. It is remarkable, moreover, that the very Alexandrian-oriented second Council of Constantinople equated "synthesis" and "hypostasis" (DR 424). Thus we can say that everything about the Son, even in his pre-existence, must be interpreted only in connection with the concrete God-man.

It is now only a matter of drawing a conclusion from this association, namely, that what is contained in scripture, tradition, and the teaching magisterium on the divine and pre-existent person of the Son can never be in conflict with what is preached about Jesus Christ. Thus it cannot be in conflict with the most primary views on Christ, which we have previously stated, that he is one person and that he is a human person. *What is said of the pre-existent divine person can never nullify this one and human person.* We must then never conceive the divine person as added to the man Jesus in such a way that Christ would no longer be one, or no longer man. But what does this mean? No Trinity and no God-man? On the contrary, as we shall see.

Where God's Trinity and especially the divine person of the Word are concerned, we must first establish that we do not know the Trinity outside its revelation, and that this revelation occurs in the Word that is flesh and in the Spirit which is poured out, in whom we receive the sonship with regard to the God and Father of Jesus Christ. In the "salvific-economic Trinity" we know the "immanent Trinity" (that is, the in-God-immanent and thus for us transcendent Trinity). Outside this revelation we do not know it. Of God insofar as he transcends his salvific operations and thus his revelation we know nothing unless it can be concluded from his work of salvation. Furthermore, we can merely say of his transcendence that it makes his work of salvation possible and not impossible. Let us apply this to God's Trinity. Can we say that God, insofar as he transcends his self-giving and self-revelation in Christ and in the Spirit given to us, thus in his "pre-existence" with regard to these salvific mysteries and with regard to all the world (pre-existence here meaning not a temporal precedence, but as merely a temporal image for transcendence)—can we say that God in this transcendence is "already" threefold? There are many who conclude to a pre-existent Trinity from the divinity of Christ and of the Spirit sent to us but they do so consciously or unconsciously via a concept of

God's immutability that is open to criticism. Thus we do not consider it justified, from this viewpoint to say that God is "already" threefold in his pre-existence. But it is just as unjustified to deny the pre-existent Trinity for this too is not contained in God's revelation in his salvific economy. What we can say regarding a pre-existent Trinity has already been negatively expressed, that is, that in any case the presence or absence of the pre-existent Trinity does not nullify the one and human person of Jesus Christ. Positively this means that we are referred to God's Trinity as it appears in Jesus Christ and the Spirit sent to us. But in Christ and the outpoured Spirit it is then also God himself who is threefold (or has become so, with a divine becoming, in which he himself changes in relation to his creatures, he himself becomes more *our* God). By virtue of this view the Christian may say that he knows God in no way other than as he has ultimately communicated himself in Jesus and in the Spirit. God is or "becomes" from his eternity, that is, from his deepest essence, the one who is for us Father, Son, and Spirit. He is on his way to this in all his essence, he has decided from the depths of his heart to be so.[16]

16. On a divine "becoming," I take the liberty of repeating what I have written in an earlier article, "Christus zonder tweeheid," *Tijdschrift voor Theologie* 6 (1966), 289–306; I posited there a real change in God by virtue of God's real relations to us and justified this as follows:

The whole of scholastic theology is opposed to the acceptance of real relations of God to his creatures, which would really determine God. The thesis of scholastic theology is that relations between God and the creature are real only from the point of view of the creature. From the side of God to creature, however, the relations are not real, but exist only in our minds (they are *"relationes rationis tantum"*). To the contrary, I believe with several other authors that we also can and must think of the relations of God to the creature as real. See, for example, E. Schillebeeckx, "De zin van het menszijn van Jesus, de Christus," in *Ts. v. Theol.* 2 (1962), 127–172, especially p. 130. We *can* think of them as real, if we eliminate the false supposition that any relation includes dependence. Of course, any relation is dependent on the term to which it is directed, for without this it cannot exist, just as it cannot exist without a subject of which it is relation. In itself, however, this is a purely logical dependence. Whoever denies the reality of relations of God to creature presupposes, moreover, that relations rest on a real dependence, on the subject of the relation becoming perfect through its term. Then, however, equality would not constitute a real relation, but only inequality, and indeed in such a way that only the relation of the lesser to the more is real and not vice versa. Scholasticism itself transcends such an outlook in its doctrine of the

Let us apply this more closely to the relation of God the Son or the Word to the man Jesus Christ. We are aware of this Word only in connection with Christ who, however, has his pre-history in the

Trinity, precisely for the relations of the divine persons *to one another*. It calls real not only the relations of the Son and the Spirit to the Father, relations in which one can see a "dependence" (albeit a divine dependence), but also the relations of the Father himself to Son and Spirit. The Father himself, however, as "source of the whole Godhead," is, in relation to the two other divine persons, not dependent in any way whatever, not receiving, but only active and bestowing. Thus scholasticism itself recognizes a purely active relation. And it must do so, if all the acting and bestowing is not to be an immanence without going out to the other. This latter is also the reason why the relations of God to the creature, if they can have such, *must* also be explained in a real way. Otherwise we are wronging the whole of the salvific message of God as our Creator and redeemer, wronging the message that he wishes to be our God. It is then an unnecessary reduction, and thus an undermining, of the good news that God is our Creator, that he loves us and enters into union with us, that the Son of God is our fellow man and suffers through and for us, if the thus expressed relation is real only in us and not in God. This is not to deny that the words on God's joy, sorrow, compassion, wrath, and even remorse, as these in particular figure in the Old Testament, are anthropomorphism and metaphorical language. God's involvement with us, however, which is indicated by these images, still remains fully real. The same holds even more for the summary which is given in the New Testament of God's work of salvation: "God is love" (I John 4, 8. 16). This love is, with regard to us, not *"rationis tantum"*!

God's real relations with us entail that change, emergence, and becoming must also be recognized in God, albeit in a completely divine way. St. Thomas never ceases to deny the possibility of change in God, and P. den Ottolander has summarized such pronouncements of Thomas in an impressive way (*Deus immutabilis. Wijsgerige beschouwing over onveranderlijkheid an veranderlijkheid volgens de theo-ontologie van Sint Thomas en Karl Barth*, Assen 1965, pp. 3–78). I completely subscribe to everything that Thomas and den Ottolander say on this point. They speak constantly of a change which rests on the individual incompletion of the changing subject, on the transition from potency to act, on growth in the broadest sense of the word. This all must indeed be excluded from our concept of God, if we wish God to be seen as God. We are also forced to this conclusion by the above-mentioned anathematism of Nicea, which excludes any change in the Son which is synonymous with creaturehood (Denz. 54 [126]), as also Vatican I, which indicates God as being a "completely unique and inalterable spiritual substance" (Denz. 1782 [3001]), and excludes from him a pantheistic self-development (Denz. 1804 [3024]). But as such a change is excluded, one question still remains which is not put by Thomas in this form and is, alas, answered too hastily by den Ottolander in the negative. This question is whether God does not change and indeed must change insofar as he is relational, whether

84

Old Testament and in all human history. Apart from this history and from the whole creation, everything that we have just said of the Trinity of God in general is valid of the Word. In connection

he does not really change in his real relations to his creatures. I answer to this in the affirmative, as also does Karl Rahner in the formula "God changes in the Other" (Karl Rahner, *loc. cit.,* note 10, p. 181). See F. Malmberg, *Über den Gottmenschen,* Basel, 1960, pp. 62–65). Again, God does not change or is not changed for his own fulfillment: this Thomist and Catholic doctrine is here not only not denied, but always assumed. But we are also saying too little if we make him a mover who himself always remains unmoved. He moves in his movements, he changes in the causing of being and becoming of the reality outside himself, and he does so in a totally divine way, without compulsion or influence, from freedom, from love. The reason which forces us to assume such a change in God lies in the very reality of his relations. He becomes different for us, he "appears differently" with regard to us, but he does so himself. Whoever thinks that his divine perfection is denied through the assumption of such a reality of God's relations and self-movements must ask himself whether the perfection which he acknowledges of God is in reality an infinite perfection, a perfection which is open to surprises and not limited *a priori* and encircled by *our concept of* perfection.

From this point of view it is not impossible that God becomes Trinity through communicating himself in a total way to, and being present in, the man Jesus as Word, and through being in the Church as Spirit. This means a becoming Trinity of God himself, thus a possession of divine hypostases in God's own being. God's Trinity is not thus, in a Sabellian or purely functionalistic way, reduced to three roles "played" by God, or to three phases of our salvific history. The inwardly becoming Trinity of God is not brought about from outside, it is not caused by men, not even by the man Jesus, who previously did not exist at all in or outside the hypostasis of God's Word. It is God himself who pronounces his Word totally in order to comprise and bear Jesus in all his dimensions, thus also from his first human origin.

Revising the English translation of this book I find myself in full agreement with these words, written in 1966, and I wish to add some other considerations:

(a) St. Thomas seems to reject real relations of God to his creatures precisely for the reason that for him (as for Aristotle) relation is an accident. This does not mean that he rejects a substantial relatedness of God to his creatures. I owe this remark to William Finan of the Aquinas Institute of Dubuque, Iowa.

(b) The assumption that God is really related and changing or becoming is in agreement with modern Anglo-Saxon thinking, especially in "process" philosophy and theology. See Alfred N. Whitehead, *Process and Reality. An Essay to Cosmology,* Cambridge, 1929; and Charles Hartshorne, *The Divine Relativity. A Social Conception of God,* New Haven, 1948; 4th ed., 1968. With process theologians I see in such a "process thought" a "resource" for Christian theology, as appears from what I wrote in the with the incarnation, however, one can conceive either a Word existing from eternity that is directed to his becoming flesh, or a Word that originates only through becoming flesh, a *Verbum incarnandum* or merely a *Verbum incarnatum*. According to the above cited principles we cannot decide in favor of one of these two possibilities. Moreover, it is pointless to ask whether the Word in God existed before the incarnation: in God there is no time. But we can speak of "before" and "after" insofar as God is concerned in our history, or rather: insofar as he refers himself to our history. We can then say that for us God's Word or God's only-begotten Son exists not only in Jesus Christ but also originates in the latter's pre-history. Whatever there is of its transcedent or pre-existent or eternal existence with God, the Word begins its existence as concerned with us in the pre-history of Jesus, when God speaks many times and in many ways to the fathers. The Prologue of St. John describes this as a self-communication and enlightenment of the Word, while Justin sees it as a history of limited participation and of preparation for his appearance as man.[17]

article quoted above. I wish to emphasize, however, that God's "becoming" is in no sense univocal to a becoming by which a created being grows, evolves, and increases. It is only by giving, bestowing, creating that God is related and that he becomes or changes. This I found best expressed in the book of Eulalio Baltazar, *God Within Process*, New York, 1970.

(c) As far as I know none of the process theologians has applied his theory to the doctrine of God's Trinity. I myself am convinced that the idea of God becoming triune through his salvific self-communications is possible. Therefore, I can go further than Karl Barth, who refers God's Trinity to a decision of God which, however, is a "primordial decision" (*"Urentscheidung,"* *Kirchliche Dogmatik I/1*, p. 404; see E. Jüngel, *Gottes Sein ist im Werden*, Tübingen, 1965). I can see God becoming triune by a historical decision of himself. This is what *we* know about God's Trinity. This vision, however, cannot be absolutized by saying that God "originally" was not triune. On a Trinity in God from eternity and by necessity we as creatures cannot make any statements, either in the affirmative or in the negative.

17. Here let it be further noted that the positing of the same personal distinction between Father and Son "before" the becoming man as afterwards, gives to the message that "God has sent his Son" the tinge of: he did not come himself, which is not in agreement with Jesus' words in John, that in him is the Father. For this latter reason the sending of Jesus by the Father is either something that happens during Jesus' earthly life or a sending into ($\epsilon \iota \varsigma$) the world (John 3, 17), by which the love of the Father prevents us from thinking that the Father "remains behind," or waits for a sacrifice brought by the Son, or is being offered satisfaction.

Let us now finally discuss the Word that is man, Jesus Christ. What must we say of him in the light of the principles developed here? In fact, no more than that we know the divine person in him only as he is at the same time fully man. For that reason the formula of Chalcedon, that the same Jesus Christ is fully God and fully man, can be further elaborated by saying that he is divine person and human person—not by an enumeration of persons, nor by a dialogue or a covenant, but because one and the same person is both divine and human, and indeed as person. Even if one thinks that one can conclude an eternal Word from the Word become man, one must still say that this Word, through becoming man, has achieved a special personal relationship to the Father. Whoever thinks that we can affirm nothing over the pre-existent Word will say that this Word is person in Jesus through its being man, that it is divine person through being a human person. It would then be best for us to speak of Jesus Christ as a divine-human person, at least if we do not find it enough to indicate his person merely by his names. We called the theory of the divine kenosis an inverted Monophysitism. The concept developed here regarding Christ's being-person is a reversal of the Chalcedonian pattern insofar as it is influenced by neo-Chalcedonism, which has become our current christology. Now not the human but the divine nature in Christ is anhypostatic, with the proviso, moreover, that this is valid inasmuch as we do not know the person of the Word outside the man Jesus. However, it is primarily not the human nature which is enhypostatic in the divine person, but the divine nature in the human person. We consider this reversal justified by our thought process to date, but some arguments can still be added. On the whole we can name three reasons for this reversal.

1. The single personality of Christ and His human personhood force us to this conception of his divine personhood, which on the other hand can be united with the data concerning such divine personhood as we hope to have demonstrated.

2. Not merely from a hermeneutic but also for an ontological viewpoint this enhypostasia of God's Word or only Son in the human person of Jesus is more obvious than the opposite, current

view. For personhood first of all is said of the man. There it has the perfection of being of the existing-in-itself, culminating in consciousness and freedom, but at the same time the limitation of individuality. If we speak of personhood in God, we must deny this limitation. Consequently, the perfection of personhood, which we must acknowledge to God, transcends our concepts. For that reason it is not the personhood itself which becomes problematical in God, but the existence of still other persons in God, opposed to his original personhood, as the Son (and the Holy Spirit) to the Father. For if an opposition in God still persists, and not in a thought construction but in reality, then it is obvious that this occurs through a limitation, and thus there cannot be a limitation in God except insofar as he identifies himself with a creature. On the one hand, then, as we argued above, a merging of the human person in a divine person through a real anhypostasia or "ecstasy of being" would nullify human personhood. On the other hand, the self-identification of God's being with a human person brings about precisely in God himself a new person and thus a plurality of persons. This view is not presented as an ontological "proof" for our concept, but rather as something that, together with our hermeneutical considerations, gives it greater probability.

3. Finally, this probability is increased still more by the expectation that our concept will remove the antinomies in current christology. Thus the question of whether Christ, besides the natural sonship, still has an adoptive sonship becomes superfluous, for there is only one sonship. This sonship can, however, be called divine, for in the man Jesus God has an Only-Begotten, but more completely it is called a God-human sonship, for it exists through the manhood of this Only-Begotten. Thus the biblical concept of "Son of God," which is formed from the basis of the people and its king, is approached in a new way. Also the division between divine and human operations is avoided, as will subsequently become obvious. Above all, however, the constant choice between an Antiochian emphasis of Christ's manhood (with the danger of a Nestorian dual personality) and an Alexandrian emphasis of the unity of the divine person (with the danger of an Apollinarian decrease or Monophysitical diminishing of Christ's manhood) is surmounted.

Such a way of overcoming a problem is not a sign of poverty but a clarification, in part because we are brought closer to the biblical christology. We hope that this will become obvious in our further elaboration.

Our concept could now be called the theory of the enhypostasia of the Word. Or in other words: of the presence of God's Word, or of God through his Word, in Jesus Christ, and indeed in such a way that this Word enters him wholly, that it becomes in him a historical person, that it becomes flesh. The second part of this sentence is indispensable, for here an attempt is made to elaborate the peculiar character of God's presence, or of the presence of God's Word, precisely in Christ. In the epistle to the Colossians this presence is described as that of God's fullness, of all his fullness: "For in him all the fullness of God was pleased to dwell" (1, 19); "for in him dwells the whole fullness of deity bodily" (2, 9). It is possible that this Fullness ($\pi\lambda\acute{\eta}\rho\omega\mu\alpha$) includes not only the fullness of God's being, but also that of the world. This can also be of service to us, but for the moment it is important that here too certainly, and primarily, the fullness of the Godhead is under discussion. This dwells in Christ and indeed, as both texts say, wholly. In the second text this dwelling is presented as "bodily" ($\sigma\omega\mu\alpha\tau\iota\kappa\hat{\omega}s$), and we could then say: in corporeality, embodied, incarnated. Thus both texts bring the same message concerning God's presence in Jesus as that contained in St. John's prologue. If in these texts the *whole* Fullness is mentioned, then this suggests that the Fullness can also partially inhabit. Of course, the distinction between "whole" and "partial" does not refer to the Godhead as such, but to its inhabitation and thus to our participation. The idea from Colossians can then be complemented by Justin's concept that the Logos was partially imparted before Christ by the appearance of the Light in the darkness from the St. John Prologue (1, 5) and by God's partial speaking to the Fathers before he spoke to us in the Son (Hebrews 1, 1). Jesus Christ is thus the crowning of God's preceding announcement of salvation, a crowning, however, which is not a fortuitous terminal point or even a relative culmination, but a genuine fulfillment, which brings the fullness of what was at first only partially given. But this does not mean that Christ comes to stand on a lonely height, for the work of salvation is directed to men: "you have come to fullness of life in him" (Colossians 2, 10), "that you may be filled with all the fullness of God" (Ephesians 3, 19). The dwelling of God's Fullness in Christ appears to be, in comparison with other texts, a terminal point, but in its own context it is rather a beginning and a point of departure. The Fullness of the Godhead, which previously had communicated itself only partially, dwells wholly in him, in order that we are fulfilled "with all the Fullness," that is, until this whole Fullness becomes ours.

Criticism of the Chalcedonian pattern has led us back to scripture. We have come from the enhypostasia of the humanity in the Word to the enhypostasia of the Word in the man Jesus Christ. We have not considered a possible existence of a divine hypostasis of the Word or of the Son outside Christ. It was exclusively a matter of God's presence in this Man, who thereby is God's only-begotten Son. This confronts us with a considerable task, that is, to indicate the *trenscendence of the Son of God precisely in his manhood*. This task is by no means a new one. The christology of the New Testament already fulfilled it, speaking in the categories of Judaism and Hellenism. But as in later reflection the two-nature pattern came to prevail, the danger of removing transcendence and the salvific meaning of Christ precisely from his human nature became correspondingly greater. One need not worry then about Jesus' humanity, seeing that the second person of God's Trinity stands "behind it" with his divine nature. Christ can be a "common" man, for he is "moreover still" God's Son.[18] Such a—mostly concealed—concept seems to be the Anselmian satisfaction theory, according to which Christ as man, through his suffering, offers satisfaction to the Father and as God bestows an infinite worth on this satisfaction. It must be emphasized, however, that in preaching and theology the individual, the transcendent, the salvific element of Christ's humanity is never forgotten. It has come to us in particular from Alexandrian theology, for whom Christ's flesh is "instru-

18. See A. Hulsbosch, "Jesus Christus, gekend als mens, beleden als Zoon Gods," in *Tijdschrift voor Theologie* 6 (1966), 250–272, esp. p. 262. This article is followed by reflections of E. Schillebeeckx and P. Schoonenberg. A survey of these three articles is given by R. North, "Soul-Body Unity and God-Man Unity," in *Theological Studies* 30 (1969), 27–60. The same author proposes a methodological reflection in "Recent Christology and Theological Method," in *Continuum* 7 (1969), 63–77.

ment of (his) divinity" and for that reason "life-giving." Here, however, the personal decisions of the human person Jesus Christ are lacking, and it is our task to illustrate his transcendence and salvific meaning precisely in them. This can rightly be called a "christological humanism." But just as there are an "atheistic humanism" and an "integral humanism," so two forms of christological humanism are also possible. For a "Godless" christological humanism is conceivable—and not merely conceivable—in which the divine sonship is simply done away with: the two-nature pattern is here simply halved.[19] But from all our foregoing reflection there is also the possibility of an "integral" christological humanism, which places the divine sonship *in* the man Jesus, a humanism that the epiphany of the Godhead sees itself achieving in manhood, that this Man sees as God's complete diaphany. We shall now attempt to give a further elaboration of *this* christological humanism.

The Human Transcendence of Jesus Christ as a Man

Let us begin with some further formal descriptions in order that we can then proceed to the content. Our christology could be called a christology without duality, a christology of God's presence, or a christology of human transcendence and salvific meaning. The elaboration of the latter in particular forms an introduction to the points in which Jesus Christ is transcendent: his relation to God and to us.

CHRISTOLOGY WITHOUT DUALITY

This title does not mean to deny a duality or complexity in Christ that is proper to man. One can wonder in anthropology, even within a Christianly inspired anthropology, whether the distinction between soul and body has meaning, and if so what, but this question has nothing to do with the christological problem that we are con-

19. An even more "godless" christological humanism is that of authors who deny that the whole idea of God (also of God the Father) can be absent from the Christian message. Dietrich Ritschl in Chapter IV of *Memory and Hope* (New York, 1967) speaks of "Atheistic Christology" (quotation marks his), referring to Herbert Braun and Paul van Buren. The latter, as far as his book *The Secular Meaning of the Gospel* (New York, 1963) is concerned, is not atheistic but rather agnostic.

cerned with here. It is, at least theoretically, possible to explain the difference between the spiritual soul and the body in all ways as a surmounted Platonic dualism, and yet to see the duality of natures in Christ as the only possible expression of his divine sonship. On the other hand, it is possible to assume a certain opposition between spiritual person and body in the man and yet to subscribe to the above criticism of the two-nature pattern. If this criticism is here further elaborated in the direction of the unity, our intention is nonetheless to surmount a duality between the divine and the human, not a possible duality or complexity within the human itself. Here too again it is only a matter of two natures which would belong to one person. It is by no means our intention to deny or to confuse the distinction between the creation and its transcendent God, not even within Christ. On the contrary, this is here greater than it would be in two-nature christology, for now it is not the fullness of his own person, but that of his God and Father, which dwells in Christ. It is then a matter of superseding the two natures of the one person by a paramount presence of God in this human person.

The same can be said concerning Christ's actions. The proceedings of the third Council of Constantinople on the two operations and wills in Christ must be interpreted in the same way as those of Chalcedon. As Chalcedon, on the basis of Nicea, spoke against Monophysitism, so Constantinople III, on the basis of the same Nicea, spoke against that Monophysitism which limited itself to the operation or the will of Christ: Monoenergetism and Monothelitism. As Chalcedon salvaged the human *being* of the Son by ascribing to him, beside his divine nature, a human nature as well, so Constantinople rescued his human *operations* by ascribing to him, besides his divine operations and will, also a human operation and will. However, if we are to conceive the divine person of the Word with his divine nature as the total presence of God in Jesus' human person, then this also holds for his human actions. There is, then, a human action and a human will and decision in Jesus Christ: this was the main subject for concern of Constantinople III. But this is totally fulfilled by God, brings God's presence to expression and communicates it, and is therefore salvific. We may not therefore ascribe a divine action to Christ that is opposed to his human actions: a creation of the world, while he as man is a dependent creature. Much rather is the Creator present in his human being and actions in such a way that this human element is itself salvific for all creation, that this man is the mediator between God and men (1 Timothy 2, 5), that in him all things have their being and in his human blood heaven and earth are reconciled (Colossians 1, 16. 20).

CHRISTOLOGY OF GOD'S PRESENCE

We have been constantly confronted thus far with the more positive characteristic of our christology: it is a *christology of God's presence,* of his *total* presence. This does not mean that elsewhere only parts or attributes of God are present, but that elsewhere it is not the whole man that is penetrated by God's presence. In Christ, however, this is precisely the case: the fullness of the Godhead has penetrated him, it dwells in him "bodily" (Colossians 2, 9), it is embodied in him. God's communicating Word has in him "become flesh" (John 1, 14). It was then necessary for the adoption-christology of the New Testament to be supplemented by an incarnation-christology. God's Fullness or Word or Spirit had to have come over Jesus, for example, during his baptism in the Jordan, and since then to have rested in him and fulfilled him. But if God fulfills this man in all his dimensions, then he does so from his origin. The two patterns of presenting this origin, that of his being conceived by the Holy Spirit and that of the Word that became flesh in him, are thus necessary, for without these images we should see in Jesus no more than one who is called, who was first far from God, someone over whom the Spirit came only later. Everything that we have just criticized in the idea of a pre-existent Word of God therefore merely referred to the concept that this Word was already there in his pre-existent person, and indeed in such a way that such an existence conflicts with his human being-person. It does not concern the incarnation itself, which says that this Man in everything (thus also in his first origin) is from God.

Here too for more concreteness we have to look at Christ's actions. There is no human action in Christ that is separated from the influence of God's presence. He does not thus have a "nature" which precedes as mere presupposition the merciful encounter with God.

93

Still less does he have a sinful existence from which he must first be freed. Nor must we distinguish in him a sphere of merely human actions, such as eating, from a God-human action. It would be a mistake to do this even in the concept which ascribed to him a pre-existent divine person, for even then any actions must emanate from this person, this person must bear it and express himself in it in one way or other. All the more, then, will the whole fullness of the Godhead penetrate any action of him in whom it dwells bodily. Certainly, this permeation, and thus its salvific meaning for us, cannot be present in every action of Christ in the same way and to the same degree. This is so, however, because not every action of Jesus, or of any man for that matter, is in the same way and to the same degree *human*. Thus Christ was not only a child, but he has, as adult, communicated the wealth of his person; he not only realized the kingdom of God by his service to men as carpenter, but also expressed it as teacher and prophet. He has not only shared our fellowship by eating with us, but has given us through bread and wine fellowship with his body and blood, as these were given and shed for us.

CHRIST'S HUMAN TRANSCENDENCE AS A MAN

Our christology without duality is thus a christology of God's complete presence in the whole man Jesus Christ. It is at the same time, therefore, christology of Jesus' transcendence as a man. As we have already said, transcendence, and thus the salvific meaning of Christ, lie now no longer in a divine person who bears his human nature, but in this human nature and above all in this human person himself. Thus their being the content of a proclamation of salvation and thus of a statement of faith and of a mystery is not lessened. Mystery is, however in the Pauline and Christian concept, not a secret doctrine on God's being insofar as this is inaccessible to common mortals, but a decree for our salvation that is now announced to anyone who faithfully accepts it: "the mystery hidden for ages and generations but now made manifest to his saints," namely, "Christ in you, the hope of glory" (Colossians 1, 26–27). That God comes to us in human ways does not mean that his presence and the bearers of his presence are no less mysterious. That we are concerned here with a statement of faith is also obvious from the fact that Christ's human transcendence is not provable in an objectifiable way, nor even demonstrable. That Jesus precisely does something that no one else can do is not clear from any of the miracle narratives in the gospel, although for someone who is open to Jesus' person he is the greatest miracle in all these narratives. That he suffered more than any other man cannot be objectifiably established. That he is without sin can be accepted only by one who has yielded to the honesty and purity of his person. Further, Jesus' human transcendence is valid for all of his existence, and thus is realized in his earthly history and at the same time in his glory, which latter is accessible only for faith.

We have said that Jesus' human transcendence is not demonstrable, that one can nowhere demonstrate anything objectifiable that is to be found only in Jesus and in no one else. If we look at Jesus' geographical and historical situation, we meet primarily with limitations: he was not a scholar, not a systematic philosopher, not an inventor, not a politician;[20] the world events of his time are not deflected from their normal course because of him. He was not living in Rome or Alexandria but in the small towns of Galilee, and in Jerusalem his failure became definitive. Jesus did not rise above the cultural, scientific, and technical achievements of his people. He was also the heir of their religious views and attitudes. That God's many and various ways of speaking via the prophets finds its culmination in the Son (Hebrews 1, 1), can be affirmed only by seeing this Son primarily as one of the prophets and as one of the teachers. A Jewish expert on the New Testament, David Flusser, once said that "we can assemble the gospel by reading the prophets and rabbis." But he added: "without *the* gospel such an anthology is impossible." Precisely in his equality with his people and with all our human race is this valid of Jesus: "No man ever spoke like this man" (John 7, 46), just as he, in the similarity between his miracles and those of others, did "works which no one else did" (John 15, 24).

20. According to the seventeenth-century course of theology known as the Salmanticenses (tract. XII, disp. 22, dubium 2, no. 29) Jesus was the greatest philosopher, the greatest poet, the greatest mathematician, and so on. It would be more true to say that in him was *something* of a philosopher, a poet, and even of—a harlequin. See Harvey Cox, *The Feast of Fools,* Cambridge, 1969, pp. 139–157.

If we further consider the difficulty of indicating and localizing Christ's transcendence in something definite, its hiddenness in the similarity with others, then we can find the reasons for this state of affairs both in the presence of God and in Jesus' manhood. Our understanding of God and man gives us an expectation of Christ; but only the concrete Christ who is Jesus fully gives us this understanding of God and man. God, as he reveals himself as Yahweh, is who he is, as he is, as he wishes to be for his people, in ways which are not ours. He finds pleasure not primarily in sacrifices but in mercy; he makes himself known not exclusively or primarily in ways of religiosity, but in ways of humanity. Precisely because everything is his creation, he reveals himself not beside the world, not by interventions exclusive of his creatures, but through bringing this creation to fulfillment. This is so most of all in man, whom he has created in his image and called to be his imitator as beloved child. For that reason the human as such is the place of God's appearance and at the same time of his hiddenness.

The human itself also makes it difficult to demonstrate Christ's transcendence. It binds men while it differentiates them: his manhood distinguishes and makes communion in the same measure. Certain differentiations or specializations make their bearer first a lofty and lonely figure and by detours fruitful for the community: the genius and the hero challenge their fellow men much more than meet them. But the most profound aspect of manhood is love, which surpasses all: the heroism to deliver his body to death by fire, all prophecy, all knowledge and insight, but which also makes fellowship by bearing all things, believing all things, hoping for all things (1 Corinthians 13). Jesus is not a genius (although "greater than Solomon" in wisdom: Matthew 12, 42), neither is he primarily a hero (although his prayer on the Mount of Olives is a heroic deed to the degree that it lacks glory), but a holy man, "the Holy One of God" (Mark 1, 24), "the Holy and Righteous One" (Acts 3, 14). But he is not a holy man who is out of the ordinary: "the Son of man came eating and drinking" (Matthew 11, 19), but one made holy by God's truth and trust, the one who sanctifies himself for others (John 17, 17), in a word: the holy one of love. For this reason the New Testament saw the fulfillment of the ideal figures of Yahweh's Servant in Jesus, he who goes meekly to men and gives himself for the many, and of the Son of man, in whom God's plan with man is fulfilled.

CHRIST, THE ESCHATOLOGICAL MAN

If Christ's transcendence is thus fully situated in the human, it becomes difficult to give an answer to such questions as: Does he differ essentially from other men or only accidentally? Is his transcendence absolute or relative? That Christ differs essentially from other men is a misleading contention, for it threatens to place him outside mankind, it threatens to annihilate the "one in substance with us" of Chalcedon. Even if we say that precisely Christ's holiness or fullness of grace differs essentially from ours, the same misunderstanding threatens. It appears then that a different holiness is given to us, while we have received precisely of his fullness, and he has given us power to become children of God (John 1, 12. 16). Moreover, one can wonder whether holiness is a completion of being-man, if Christ differed from us essentially in the first but not in the second. Thus the term "essentially" does not appear to be a suitable indication of the difference between Christ and us. But must this difference then be called accidental? But this latter term does not sufficiently express Christ's transcendence with regard to all and therefore his salvific meaning for all. Roughly the same can be said with regard to "absolute" and "relative." Certainly, the second term says too little. It places Jesus in the same category as the religious geniuses and the prophets, in relation to whom he is precisely God's completing word. For that reason he can be called an absolute culmination, but then within manhood and within the human history of salvation.[21]

In order to express the latter we would have to use a more specifically theological and also scriptural term, that is, *"eschatological."*

21. The question which we deal with in this section in modern Anglo-Saxon theology is usually formulated this way: Does Christ differ from us in kind or in degree? Valuable answers have been given by process theologians as Peter Hamilton, *The Living God and the Modern World,* Philadelphia, 1967, pp. 208–210; Norman Pittenger, *Christology Reconsidered,* London, 1970, pp. 111–133. These authors opt for a difference in degree but so that Christ completes and perfects God's saving work in the world. On their conception of eschatology see further on, note 68.

Jesus Christ is the eschatological culmination of God's salvific operations and thus of our history of salvation. God speaks through him to us "in these last days" (Hebrews 1, 2) or "to the end of the ages"; therefore, "the end of the ages has come" to us (1 Corinthians 10, 11). But the early Church was forced to relinquish the expectation of an imminent parousia, and not only has history continued after Jesus Christ but our faith tells us that in some way or other it must now also be salvific history. For that reason the eschatological element of Christ's position should be understood much more qualitatively: in the history of salvation he is *definitive,* God's complete Word, speaking and further expressed in "the fullness of time" (Galations 4, 4; see Mark 1, 15). But the end of the ages is not lacking in the eschatological character of Christ, for we profess him not merely as the Jesus who once lived but also as the "first-fruits of those who have fallen asleep" (1 Corinthians 15, 20), as "first-born from the dead" (Colossians 1, 18). He already stands in the final completion and from there he remains for us as an example, but also as inspiration, bringer of salvation, life, freedom, love, sonship. These salvific gifts are partially ascribed to the Spirit, but this Spirit is his own. For that reason we read in St. John that the Spirit reminds us of what Jesus has said (John 14, 26), that the Spirit of Christ receives and preaches it (John 16, 14), and Paul even says that "the Lord is the Spirit" (2 Corinthians 3, 17). Christ remains, then, the completion, he remains so as the one who is himself completed. Our christology can finally be called: a *christology of the human final completion.*

JESUS AND GOD

The emphasis which has been given to the *human* transcendence and final completion of Jesus Christ causes one perhaps to expect that we will now elaborate it in its content alone for Jesus' relations to mankind. This aspect of his person, his freedom to love, naturally finds most sympathy with the secularized man of today. In a writer such as Paul van Buren Jesus' relation to God is ignored because according to him one cannot affirm or deny anything of God; for others Jesus is, or seems to be, purely the substitute of God, the man in whom the reality of God himself has become

world and has died our death.[22] There is not room here to render an
account of our own affirmation of God. We should only like to point
out that it is impossible for us to write a christology without assent-
ing to Jesus' God and Father as reality, indeed as the paramount
reality of his and our existence. We have every respect for linguistic
analysis and consider it a valuable aid for our exegesis of scripture
and tradition. But reduction of the religious language to no more
than a self-expression of the man, without discussing him to whom
this language is directed as a reality, does not appear to us to follow
from linguistic analysis, but from a positivism that precedes linguistic analysis.[23] And this positivism is just as unacceptable for us as a
philosophy which makes God to be absorbed in his world. Therefore, we have no reason to make objections against a personal God
and Father of Christ, as we certainly did have reason to place his
personal pre-existence in question. The personal pre-existence of the
Son can be left out of the message of the New Testament—and in
fact plays no part in the synoptic gospels—but the person of the
Father is everywhere the center.

In the gospels and in the prayers of the community we hear
Jesus' own confidential mode of address to God: Abba, Father
(Mark 14, 36; Romans 8, 15; Galatians 4, 6). For that reason Jesus
had in this community not only the messianic title "Son of God" but
also the completely personal one of "the Son" (for example, Matthew 28, 19; Hebrews 1, 2), a word which He probably used de-
scriptively of Himself (Matthew 11, 27ff.; Mark 12, 6ff.; 13, 32f.).[24]
Jesus reveals himself primarily in his message concerning the
Father's kingdom, and the explicit self-pronouncements in St. John's
gospel are also directly connected with words of Jesus on the Father.
In the gospels Jesus' prayer to the Father plays a great part: all of
them describe how, from his praying, he reached acceptance of his
suffering. Luke shows him praying at his baptism, before the calling
of the Twelve and on the transfiguration (Luke 3, 21; 6, 12; 9, 28f.),

22. On Christ as God's "representative," see Dorothee Sölle, *Representation,* London, n.d. On God's death in Christ, see Thomas J. J. Altizer,
The Gospel of Christian Atheism, Philadelphia, 1966.

23. See O. Muck, "Zur Logik der Rede von Gott," in *Zeitschrift für
katholische Theologie* 89 (1967), 1–28.

24. See B. M. F. van Iersel, *"Der Sohn" in den synoptischen Jesusworten,*
Leiden, 1961.

John anticipates the prayer for the suffering (John 12, 27f.; 17). To his disciples Jesus teaches the "Our Father," in Luke even from his own prayer (Luke 11, 1). Before we pray in this prayer for our need for daily bread and forgiveness, we have to pray for the coming of the Father's kingdom. And even before this prayer we are taught to say: "Hallowed be thy name" (Matthew 6, 9; Luke 11, 2). This is the first thing which, according to Jesus, we have to say after we have addressed God with the same name that he himself gave him: that this name be hallowed, that is, deemed holy and acknowledged as the most holy and most beloved name which can be pronounced. The self-pronouncements, the praying of Jesus and the prayer that he taught us, give us a glimpse into the consciousness that he himself had of God and of his own relation to him as Father. If we look at this consciousness more closely—if we venture to discuss the attitude of Jesus before the Father—then two characteristics strike us: clarity and immediacy.

Clarity. Jesus is not a sinner praying to God, not the lost son returning to the Father. In his own prayer the gospels do not show us the least trace of a prayer for forgiveness, not even before his death. Neither does Jesus in fact pray simply to receive God's grace. He knows himself to be without sin and living completely with God. He does pray for freedom from suffering and death on the Mount of Olives (Mark 14, 36 and par.) and also, with the words of Psalm 22, on the cross (Mark 15, 34. 37 and par.; see John 11, 41f.), and finally for his own glorification, which again is the glorification of the Father and includes the union with his own (John 17). The lack of guilt or wrong makes Jesus' prayer no less fervent; rather the opposite is the case. It makes Jesus' prayer ultimately free of all self-interest that might stand in the way of God's kingdom. God's will is his final word. This is a relationship of the highest surrender and of the most disinterested love. Our own relation to our parents is often troubled, and in many ways this has its influence on our relation to God. In the relation of Jesus to his Father there is no trace of an Oedipus complex: we can call it "psychoanalytically pure," as a theologian-psychologist has expressed it.[25] Perhaps in

25. B. Bro, "Man and the Sacraments. The Anthropological Substructure of the Christian Sacraments," in *The Sacraments in General. A New Perspective,* ed. by E. Schillebeeckx and B. Willems, New York, 1968,

these words lies a piece of gospel for our psychologically so burdened Western culture.

Besides the clarity of Jesus' relation to the Father, there is also its *immediacy*. Precisely for our Christian practice of praying through Christ, his own prayer and life strike one as an immediate relationship with the Father.[26] But we must be careful with this characterization. A relationship which is merely immediate can be assumed only by those who accept an eternal divine person in Christ, and then only for this divine person in his divine nature. But one must also then speak of Jesus' human relationship to God, for it is only through his humanity that Jesus' relationship to the Father is expressed and becomes salvific. One comes, then, to this question: How far can the relationship of this man to God be called immediate? Actually, the distinction between mediate and immediate is not suitable for the relation between God and creature, at least insofar as God and creature are supposed to be in contact with one another "merely" by means of something between them. God reaches every creature immediately, for he realizes everything of all creatures, including their mutual relations. For that reason we always reach God in a created reality, although it is also that of ourselves, while on the other hand it is God himself whom we—immediately—reach. This immediate contact will be more eloquent according to the degree in which one opens himself to it, and we know Jesus as a man of prayer in lonely places, but also as someone who, in his daily contacts, was captivated by the Father. Such a contact has at the same time a more ontological basis according to the degree in which one, in one's own created reality, may see the fruits of a more excellent initiative of God; and precisely in this view Jesus more than anyone else could experience God in himself. Everything in which he transcends other men—in the sense in which we elaborated this point above: distinguishes himself from them and also unites himself with them—is the work and gift of the Father. This we find repeatedly expressed in the gospel of St. John: "The Son can do nothing of his own accord, but only what he sees the Father doing; for whatever he does, that the Son does likewise" (5, 19). It is thus

pp. 33–50, esp. p. 47: "the only existence that has ever been psycho-analytically pure."

26. Hulsbosch, *op. cit.* (note 18), p. 270.

also understandable how Jesus, precisely in the performance of "works" and "signs," feels the Father working in him: "Father, I thank thee that thou hast heard me" (John 11, 41). Through this immediacy Jesus is the mediator for us. But it is important to bear in mind that the concept of "mediator" was applied to Christ only late in the New Testament—in the epistle to the Hebrews (8, 6; 9, 15; 12, 24), which gives an elaborate presentation of Jesus' high priesthood, and in one of the pastoral epistles (1 Timothy 2, 5). This can serve to draw our attention to the fact that he wishes to make us sharers in the immediacy of his relation to the Father. In the synoptic gospels the kingdom of God means an immediate relationship to the Father—but it is present in Jesus. In John we trace both elements, though perhaps with the reverse accent: Jesus says: "He who has seen me has seen the Father" (John 14, 9), but also: "the Father himself loves you, because you have loved me" (John 16, 27).

JESUS' LOVE OF MANKIND

From out of this love which his Father has for everyone Jesus finds his own love for everyone. God is completely in him and reveals himself in him as love to us. The most remarkable characteristic of this love is that it knows no bounds. It breaks through the "closed morality" which are so peculiar to our manhood and especially to our sinfulness.[27] The breakthrough of such a limited love of one's "neighbor" already happened before for us and exists outside the Christian world and probably forms the best proof of God's presence. Israel knows the care of Deuteronomy not only for the widow and orphan but also for "the sojourner within your towns"; but this thought is contradicted in the Old Testament by the enmity against the nations inside and outside Canaan and the many particular enmities in which the Israelite asks Yahweh to intervene with both parties as judge. One calls to mind here the series of prophecies against the nations, and the psalms, or passages from the psalms, in which prayers are offered that disaster befall the enemy. In this sense it is not strange to find in Matthew 5, 43 that the words from Leviti-

27. The "closed morality" is classically described by Henri Bergson in *The Two Sources of Morality and Religion*, New York, 1954.

cus 19, 18: "you shall love your neighbor," are amplified by "and hate your enemy." It is, however, mainly a matter of what Jesus follows this with: "But I say to you, love your enemies and pray for those who persecute you, so that you may be sons of your Father who is in heaven" (Matthew 5, 44f.). This ideal is demonstrated most aptly in the parable of the Good Samaritan, which is an answer to the question, "Who is my neighbor?" (Luke 10, 29–37). These are all words of Jesus; that it is also the way he acts appears particularly from his association with publicans and sinners (Mark 2, 15–17 and par.). It is specifically this association with publicans and sinners which is justified by the parables of Luke 15: before narrating the parable of the searching shepherd, the searching housewife, and the merciful father, Jesus is himself the active sign of God's boundless love. One can say that Jesus' association with the sinners as revolutionary deed was one of the reasons for the enmity which brought him to the cross, and that this is the first sense in which he died for sinners.[28]

Jesus' death on the cross not only is the result of the loyalty and obedience to the mission which he had received from God his Father, to the preaching and realization of his kingdom, but it can be conceived as a sacrifice pleasing to God. The death on the cross is just as much the result of Jesus' loyalty to us, for he is sent to us. Thus it could be interpreted as the self-giving for the many of Yahweh's Servant. It is possible that Jesus himself interpreted his death in this way, especially in the words during the Last Supper on his body, which is "for you" (1 Corinthians 11, 24), "is given for you" (Luke 22, 19). Jesus' words on the cross in Luke express an attitude of pardon, intercession for forgiveness, and trusting surrender to God (Luke 23, 34–46), and show Jesus dying as he had lived. His gift to all is, in his death on the cross, a gift for all, for the benefit of all, but in celebrating the memory of his death, which is at the same time a meal with the Resurrected One, he gives himself again *to* us all. In his Spirit also the community of his believers has broken through the barriers of Judaism and extended to the heathens. His gift to all must be realized by us. The love without conditions and without boundaries, which was and is his gift, has become our task.

28. D. M. Baillie, *God Was in Christ*, London, 1960, pp. 182–184.

JESUS' FREEDOM

Those today who are convinced that the gospels do not give a description of the life of Jesus but feel that many of the pericopes show us his figure during his earthly life, see in this figure primarily his freedom and authority. For van Buren, freedom is the basic characteristic of Jesus, and he confesses himself to this man in an agnosticism towards God. For Bornkamm, authority or full power is Jesus' basic characteristic,[29] and this full power is precisely freedom by virtue of God's mission and authority. Freedom is in the first instance freedom from. We saw this already in Jesus confronted with the old law: the contrast: "You have heard that it was said to the men of old . . . but I say to you," repeated six times in Matthew 5, seems to have come inalienably from Jesus' own mouth. Jesus also took a free and independent position with regard to the ruling caste and the ruling ideas and—which says more—with regard to his kinsmen, his mother included, and finally—which says more still—with regard to those who wished to follow him and with regard to the ideas and wishes of his actual followers, such as Peter. This freedom from is a freedom to, to the mission which the Father gave him. Finally, Jesus' real kinsmen are those who do the Father's will and against Peter and against Satan; one has to be concerned not with what men want but with what God wants. The highest freedom from and freedom to, and thus the highest courage and power of Jesus—which here too shows to full advantage in weakness—is expressed in the prayer on the Mount of Olives.

It is good to remember this freedom, which is full power from God. It is the source of Jesus' love to the Father and to mankind. More than the external deeds, this freedom guarantees that Jesus' double love is boundless and unconditional. But at the same time it allows us to see how far human transcendence is accessible only for faith in the person of Jesus, as we have already said above. Only by opening oneself for his person, not by the measurment of one's achievements, could others, during Jesus' earthly life, come to this image of him, and only in the same way can we experience him now. This is much more the case now because the freedom and

29. Van Buren, *op. cit.* (note 19); G. Bornkamm, *Jesus of Nazareth,* London, 1960.

the love of Jesus are certainly audible since his death and resurrection in the word of proclamation, but visible only in the faithful themselves. We must ourselves thus make Jesus' transcendence and salvific meaning real by our faith and our life, whereas they were given to us primarily so that we might believe, and thus arouse our faith. Thus we have again arrived at the distinction between Christ's earthly and glorified life, which we shall now discuss more fully.

2. The Earthly and the Glorified Life of Christ as a Man

In our introduction to this study we emphasized the fact that the two-nature pattern says nothing about Jesus' own history, and in particular nothing on the distinction between his earthly and his glorified life. He is in both equally God's eternal Son and in both equally man. For various reasons this distinction is insufficiently elaborated in scholastic theology, and indeed practically denied: the thesis that Christ was on earth *"viator simul et comprehensor,"* earthly pilgrim and possessor of the heavenly vision, is the best proof of this fact. Theoretically, such theses are independent of the two-nature doctrine, but in practice they are affirmed on the basis of the divine person in Christ. In what follows, therefore, we will introduce some amplifications and corrections with regard to scholastic christology which were already partially possible within the two-nature pattern, but which can here be carried through more logically. They will first of all be concerned with Jesus' earthly life in general, and then with his knowledge and will in this life, while a reflection on his glorfied life forms the conclusion. Our intention is not directly to discuss the salvific meaning of the earthly life, of the death and glorification of Christ. Rather our concern will be with the period in history in which the salvific facts took place, in which the salvific decisions of Christ were made.

Jesus Inserted into History

Jesus is in history, he is inserted in it, he is "historical." This means that he is defined by our history, but also himself has his history, makes his own history and thus defines ours. We shall first examine some passive, and then the more active aspects of the "historicity" of Jesus.

JESUS' DESTINY

Jesus' existence is carried out in a situation which is defined by history. Historical decisions formed his people with their own language, culture, and religion. His family itself has its pre-history, which is recalled by the names in his genealogical tree. For Jesus this situation makes some things possible and others impossible during his life and even ever since his origin; for his history changes and thus Jesus' possibilities also change during his life.

Any christology which seriously includes Christ's manhood will acknowledge this fact. But there is a difference between the two-nature doctrine and our own precisely in the seriousness with which Jesus' life situation is conceived. If one assumes that the same person who on earth is Jesus of Nazareth has existed from eternity as divine person, then it is possible to say that this person himself chooses or "has chosen" the situation in which he has to live as a man. Then the life situation for the human existence of Jesus can be called a destiny, but for his divine person it is the object of an eternal choice. The Son of God chooses, then, or "has chosen," to be our companion in destiny, but through this individual choice, "destiny" for him has a different content than for us. We encounter such an idea in mariological treatises and pious contemplations on Jesus' mother. There the Son of God is the only one who chooses his own mother, a point of departure from which conclusions are occasionally drawn concerning Mary's grace. In particular we encounter such a view where texts on Jesus' emptying of himself, especially Philippians 2, 66, are theologically elaborated. Then the emptying becomes a choice of the preexistent Son in his becoming man, which however does not exclude the fact that it can also be a constant choice of Jesus during his earthly life. But it is precisely the first which we should like to exclude, not as possibility, but as theological point of departure. We have in our first part not been able to affirm or deny the personal pre-existence of the Word or the Son; for that reason it is now impossible for us to affirm or deny that God the Son himself chose his own mother, his family or people, his modest level of existence, or whatever situation of his orgin. We must radically maintain our standpoint by saying: just as there is certainly no pre-existent person of the Word *insofar* as this would nullify or lessen the actual human personhood of Jesus, so is there likewise no pre-existent choice of his own circumstances of life *insofar as* this would nullify or lessen a genuine human fate of Jesus. This is not a contradiction of what we have said previously regarding Jesus' all-surpassing and thus all-liberating freedom. Precisely as human freedom, this is a freedom in a situation, a freedom within his destiny. This precisely makes its greatness as human freedom, which may not be nullified by a divine freedom which is supposed to precede his destiny.

If Jesus' destiny is not the object of his own choice, this does not prevent it from being the object of the Father's will. In John, Jesus calls his suffering "the cup which the Father has given me" (John 18, 11). We must certainly see the will of God in all its transcendence, whereby it does not take a place among worldly causes or replace them in such a way that it should remove the fortuitousness or contingency of human history. Just as little as God's will would make human freedom less free does it make our destiny less destiny. In the destiny of Jesus, therefore, there are many things which "could have happened differently." This is especially important in connection with the death on the cross, and it is to the credit of Romano Guardini to have made this emphatically clear.[30] He rightly points out the human guilt which caused Jesus' death on the cross and his human failure, which only through God's superabundant grace became his victory and our salvation.

The difficulty in accepting this contingent element in Jesus' destiny springs, moreover, from the fact that so much in Jesus' life, and especially his suffering and death, happened "in accordance with the scriptures" (1 Corinthians 15, 36; see *inter al.* Acts 3, 18; Matthew 26, 54. 56). For numerous misunderstandings lie at the foundation of such reasoning. Even if prophecy were an accurate prediction on the basis of God's foreknowledge or indeed of God's will, nothing is taken away, as we have just said, from human freedom and historical contingency. But nothing indicates that we have to do here with such a prediction in which God's foreknowledge enters the stream of our human knowledge. This is even highly im-

---

30. Romano Guardini, *The Lord,* Chicago, 1954.

probable, primarily because we may not imagine God's knowledge as an infinite "quantity" of conceptual pronouncements which simply supplement our human knowledge, and consequently because precisely such a supplementation would hardly accord with God's transcendent rule. Prophecy—insofar as it is oriented to the future—is much more the interpretation of God's salvific work as future-giving, as promise, it is orientation of our hope. For that reason the material content of the prophetic view of the future is not important, and this can always turn out differently without the prophecy losing in value as announcement of God's promise and as orientation of hope. For that reason, prophecy can be fulfilled in different periods in even different ways, as is the prophecy of Nathan or of the messianic psalms first in the kingdom of Solomon, after that in the kingdom of the glorfied Christ, and finally in his return. A prophetic text can, then, on the basis of a new situation become bearer of a new perspective of the future. Moreover, some texts from the Old Testament, especially the songs of Yahweh's Servant, give more an ideal picture than a perspective of the future, so that they create still less the necessity that what is said will one day be literally realized. Finally, we should also consider the fact that texts often become prophetic or more prophetic through the interpretation with which they are later read and transmitted. This can also happen if they are used to interpret something that *has* happened. A *"vaticinium post eventum"* in the sense of an antedated straightforward prediction is, of course, deceptive, but the use of an earlier text oriented to the future for the interpretation of something that has already happened reveals a meaning of text and event that they have in the one salvific operation of God. From all this it certainly follows that prophecies never make a literal fulfillment necessary and thereby impinge upon human freedom or historical contingency. Consequently, they no more hinder the fact that Jesus had in reality a human destiny than do God's rule in general or Jesus' divine sonship.

JESUS DESCRIBED "NON-HISTORICALLY"

Everything that comes to us from Jesus through history is also historically conditioned. The communities which believed in him and their leaders have interpreted and proclaimed him in the concepts handed down to them through their own traditions, especially through the scriptures of the Old Testament and through Judaism—within whose concepts, moreover, Jesus himself had understood and imparted his message and his person. They celebrated him and the salvation brought by him in signs which again corresponded to the traditions in which they lived and which themselves have, through a long history, assumed the form of our present sacraments. We have not only to assimilate and thus first of all to accept the history between Jesus and ourselves, but we have also to realize that we nowhere find words or institutions of the first communities, or of Jesus, which are not themselves also the fruits of a history which preceded them. This insight into the historical conditioning of everything that comes to us will bring about in us, with regard to the Christian tradition, the same attitude which man has to take up with regard to any valuable tradition, that is, the double attitude of reverence and freedom, which again is one in loyalty. We have now to interpret in freedom and translate for our times the message of and about Jesus and the forms which our Christian confession, prayer, and celebration has assumed; and they have, of course, been interpreted and translated in this way in every age. This freedom is demanded by our loyalty to what is itself handed down. A literal repetition of the message in its earlier form will render it incomprehensible, or give rise to misunderstanding, and precisely for that reason it would not be a loyal tradition. On the other hand, the first deposit of any tradition has a certain value as source for renewed inspiration. In Christ's Church this first deposit has a very special value in scripture. For that reason we should like to say a few words about the scriptures of the New Testament, precisely insofar as they share in Jesus' historicity.

Any reality is registered in our knowledge not merely in its objectivity, but it is connected with all our thought and experience and interpreted in connection with these. Our first contact with it is already defined by the necessary limitation of our interest, by the questions we ask: already we begin to interpret. What we have here written is chiefly an outlook which lies at the foundation of phenomenology and is elaborated in various forms by existential philosophy. These form a reaction to the ideal which grew in the eighteenth and nineteenth centuries of an "objective" knowledge, for which man was considered to be merely an observer, a clean slate on which the "facts" could be registered, both of natural events and of human events. It is well to realize that such an objective ideal of knowledge is very recent, even in our Western history, and that the present reaction makes us aware in a reflexive way of what is present in any human experience and was largely considered by former cultures to be self-evident. For scripture, of the Old as well as the New Testament, there is no "objective" registration in the sense of modern science. Terms such as "real" and "true" must then have had a meaning for the writers of the Old and New Testaments different from our own. For John 15, 1, Jesus is the true vine, while for us the plant which is so called is the genuine vine and Christ is a vine in a figurative sense. Although this is an extreme example, because John 15, 1 is laden with the Johannine concept of truth, it nevertheless illustrates how human interpretation in scripture can take possession of a concept which for us is primarily biological.

The concept "really happened" also has a meaning in scripture different from our own. Certainly, we are beginning to realize that no fact comes to us other than in an interpretation, but the ideal of the historical sciences still remains the reconstruction of the past by neutralizing the various interpretations of the documents. Just as we inevitably encounter nature as we have examined it but yet wish to penetrate it to find this nature "itself," so we also meet the past inevitably as examined by the present but nevertheless wish to make the past "itself" speak. But it is precisely this historical preoccupation which was foreign to the man of biblical cultures. His writing of history is always simultaneously proclamation, prophecy, in the broadest sense of the word, which is the reason why a series of "historical books" of the Old Testament are referred to as the "earlier prophets" in the Hebrew Bible and another series falls under the "The Law." In these books, especially in the historical parts of the Torah, it is not, as we might expect, the past which is first reconstructed and then interpreted for the hearer or reader. Rather the interpretation occurs in the narrative itself. That Yahweh is the source from which Israel can accomplish its history in joyful trust is expressed by "mythologically" making him participate in historical events: he leads his people with a strong arm out of

Egypt, horse and rider he throws into the sea. In the New Testament the main "historical" writings are called "gospels," that is, good news. Even more than the Old Testament historical sections, they comprise a multitude of literary forms, registered and described by the exponents of "form criticism," especially Bultmann and Dibelius. However, even more important than these individual literary genres is the genre of "gospel" itself, to which Bornkamm draws our attention.[31] Here too the believing interpretation is situated in the narration of history itself, and not added to it. This interpretation says not only that God has spoken to us in an ultimate, definitive way in the earthly life of Jesus of Nazareth, but also that he has raised and glorified this Jesus. This latter point is the most proper characteristic of the literary genre of "gospel." Gospel is consequently on the one hand the narration of Jesus' earthly life in the light of his resurrected life now for us, or on the other hand the good news of this resurrected life, expressed in the narration of deeds and words from his earthly life.

Thus the gospel belongs to the historical situation in which Jesus pronounced his message and in which the first communities developed it and wrote it down. Although a message of faith could certainly be expressed, no writing of history *in our sense* was possible. This situation continued for a long time. Although there were already in the Middle Ages some questions about "what really happened" regarding some facts in the margin of scripture (whether or not, for example, the serpent in Genesis 3 crawled on its belly before being cursed), everything in the gospels had long been considered to have "really happened" and at the same time to be a salvific event (alas, the first more often than the second). This way of thinking altered only with the Enlightenment. In our time this legacy has come to us in the "quest for the historical Jesus," which was carried out mainly in the German-speaking countries.[32] It began with the sensational essay of Reimarus, "Vom Zwecke Jesu und

31. G. Bornkamm, *op. cit.* (note 29).
32. For the history of the *Leben-Jesu-Forschung* see, *inter alia*, Albert Schweitzer, *The Quest of the Historical Jesus*, New York and London, 1963; James M. Robinson, *A New Quest of the Historical Jesus*, London, 1959; H. Ristow-K. Matthiae, *Der historische Jesus und der kerygmatische Christus*, Berlin, 1960; H. Zahrnt, *The Historical Jesus*, New York and London, 1963; J. R. Geiselmann, *Jesus der Christus I*, Munich, 1965.

seiner Jünger" ("On the Purpose of Jesus and His Disciples"), in which he made a radical division between Jesus' historical figure as unsuccessful instigator of a political-revolutionary movement and the disciples who stole Jesus' body and initiated Christianity with the narration of his resurrection. The philosopher and poet Lessing published this essay because he thought that it and similar objections would purify Christianity of its historical pretensions and cause the "general truths" therein to emerge more clearly. The idea of Christianity as (the highest form of) "a general religion" thereafter governed the liberal theology of the nineteenth century. The Jesus one thought to find by liberating him not only from Christian dogma but also from the New Testament pronouncements of faith was primarily an ethical and religious figure. He was so for Strauss, Renan, and Harnack. Albert Schweitzer at the beginning of this century brought an end to the quest for the historical Jesus, which had wanted to bring Jesus back to our time and yet had never been able to do so convincingly. Schweitzer saw Jesus as the apocalyptic prophet of a nearly coming kingdom of God, while Christianity precisely was to give this up, but could remain faithful to the attitudes of Jesus. At the same time there rose up the school of the history of religions of Wilhelm Bousset, who regarded Christianity much more as a product of Hellenistic syncretism and Paul more than Jesus as its founder.

The diversity of all these attempts should not allow us to forget that a positive element was slowly but steadily emerging: an insight into the layers of tradition which were reflected in the New Testament. Strauss made a sharp division between the synoptics and John; Harnack divided the synoptic gospels into two sources, the narrative of Mark and the source of Jesus' sayings, the *Logienquelle*; Wrede sees in St Mark's gospel itself the theology of the community already at work; the school of the history of religions has discovered —as always with that element of exaggeration common to first discoveries—the difference between the Jewish and the Hellenistic traditions in the New Testament, which was later to be refined in the (relative) differences between Palestinian-Jewish, Jewish-Hellenistic, and Hellenistic Christianity.[33] This unravelling reached a certain

33. This threefold distinction is most systematically elaborated by Ferdinand Hahn and Reginald H. Fuller (see note 1).

culmination in the schools of "form criticism" and "tradition criticism," while the theological syntheses later to the fore in "redaction criticism."[34] All of these literary investigations affirm the great influence of the interpreting communities and authors, which can be traced in almost every sentence of the gospels. Negatively, this makes it even more clear that a history of Jesus in our sense is not to be found in the gospels—and therefore nowhere. The impossibility of writing a biography of Jesus is also generally acknowledged. This does not deprive us of all possibility of establishing something about Jesus' earthly life that in our sense is historical. Methods have developed which lay bare some *"ipsissima verba,"* and in particular the various traditions have all given to us the figure of Jesus in his fullness of power and freedom to love and in his inner relation to God as his Father. But it continues to hold of Jesus' historical situation that no history of him exists in our sense of the word.[35]

It is precisely this situation which we must accept in faith. And indeed primarily in a joyful faith, which recognizes how much it must and may be faith. Bultmann was always fearful that a historical knowledge would render faith superfluous. In fact, however, what is detected by historical investigation is not an object of faith. Even if we, in our historical knowledge of Jesus, were to equal the knowledge of his contemporaries, our faith in Jesus' person and mission would be no easier, nor would it be any more difficult, for us than for them. Extensive historical knowledge need harm faith just as little as make it easier. It could indeed articulate the content of our faith more in a better way. On the other hand, however, faith itself gives us the guarantee concerning a minimum of historical content. We believe, then, not only in the possibility but in the reality of God's complete salvific presence in Jesus Christ. God *has* spoken in him and Jesus *has* existed. Bultmann by no means wished to deny the historical existence of Jesus—he even says that such a denial is not worth refuting—but it is not clear whether this historical existence itself is proclaimed in the kerygma to the faith and affirmed by the faith. Tillich thought differently. He says quite

34. See Edgar V. McKnight, *What is Form Criticism?*, Philadelphia, 1969; Norman Perrin, *What is Redaction Criticism?*, Philadelphia, 1969.
35. In Anglo-Saxon exegesis this has been made clear in a particular way by James M. Robinson (note 32).

clearly that it is our faith which affirms the complete presence of the "new being" in a man. He adds, however, that faith cannot affirm that this man precisely was Jesus of Nazareth, that it neither gives nor demands proofs of this assertion.[36] Here, however, one can ask whether the mere fact of God's complete salvation in one man, without our even knowing his name, can really be called a presence of God among men.

According to the degree in which the historical in our sense of the word appears to be less present in the books of the New Testament, it becomes clear that there is correspondingly a greater need for an interpretation of Jesus' person and meaning. If, however, one rejects the idea that the historical in our modern sense is the only "real" element—the only thing which, through a mutual neutralization of the various interpretations remains objectifiable, and which neither believer nor unbeliever can doubt—then there is likewise no foundation for asserting or suspecting that the interpretation is only "subjective." It is indeed subjective insofar as it is a deed of the interpreter, but inherent in this deed is the recognition of the meaning which the fact admits, and insofar as this is so the interpretation overcomes subjectivism. Giving meaning is also taking meaning, actively receiving and recognizing meaning.[37] In Jesus lies the foundation for recognizing him as Yahweh's Servant, as Messiah. There is such a fullness of meaning, in him, however, that more than one christology is possible, especially in the New Testament itself. This interpretive many-sidedness is apparent not only in the various christological titles, but also in the various contrasts between adoption christology and incarnation christology.

In this connection one can again nourish a false cult of the historical in the above-mentioned objectifying sense by considering that christology to be the most valuable which is the oldest—which in practice comes down to the adoption pattern. But this would be misjudging the possibility of real evolution and progress in human history. It is not honest, for example, regarding doctrine of

36. Paul Tillich, *Systematic Theology II*, New York and London, 1957. The ever possible doubt whether the Christ was precisely Jesus of Nazareth or not Tillich calls "an historically absurd, but logically necessary, consequence of the historical method" (p. 131).

37. Herman Berger, *Op zoek naar identiteit*, Nijmegen, 1968, pp. 191–211.

orginal sin, to point out the moral imperfections of the first men and then, with reference to our theme, adhere to the most primitive layer of christology. Of course, these two points are quite distant from one another, but they agree in that both in moral feeling and in the interpretation of facts and persons real progress is possible. This is still possible when the Christian proclamation passes from Judaism to Hellenism and comes to express itself in the latter's concepts. In itself Hellenistic thought need be no less valuable (and no less inadequate) than the Jewish. In any case, the Christian message *had to* embody itself in Hellenistic thought, with the same necessity with which it must now be incarnated in modern Western, Asian, or African thought. Further, the transition from the inner-scriptural to the post-biblical tradition presents no difficulty for such progress, since that the primacy of scripture with regard to post-biblical tradition is again limited by the fact that the evangelical message stands above both.[38]

The historical distance between Jesus and ourselves can then be regarded as a distinct possibility for a better christology. But we must still further elaborate the concept of evolutionary thought. All evolution is also specialization, that is, an elaboration of one determined possibility, while others are left unused. There is, however, a great difference between pre-human evolution and that which is carried out in human history. In the former the unused possibilities cannot later be used by the beings who developed in a different direction. In man this is not the case. He cannot, of course, undo the development once achieved, but he can attempt to synthesize the unused possibilities in his society and those which he himself has developed. For christology this means first of all that we must recognize the possibility and the fact of development or at least of the maintenance of a standard in the christology of Chalcedon. This was built upon the title "Son of God" and on incarnation christology. What can be said on the transcendence of Jesus Christ and at the same time on his being-man-with-us was expressed in the form then possible with great emphasis and sublimity. For that reason we must remain faithful to Chalcedon. But on the other hand, precisely the impasse of the two-nature pattern tells us that we can also conceive

38. J. Ratzinger, "The Concept of Tradition," in K. Rahner and J. Ratzinger, *Revelation and Tradition*, New York and London, 1966.

of the incarnation christology without starting from the personal pre-existence. Thereby it will admit of greater mobility and thus of a synthesis with the unutilized possibilities of adoption christology.

IN THE HISTORY OF SALVATION AND OF EVIL

Such a synthesis will emerge in particular if we come to examine the history of Jesus himself. Before doing so, however, we should like to make yet another observation on his place in history insofar as this is the history of salvation and of evil. Jesus' destiny is a destiny of salvation that had to be surpassed and of evil that had to be overcome. As completion of God's history of salvation, Jesus Christ is also included therein. He is also heir to that which he completes. He is from Israel according to the flesh, but this flesh includes a history of faith, a culture of prayer, a tradition, and a scripture. Israel, however, is called from among the nations and owes its liturgy to Canaan and its wisdom to the whole of the Near East. Thus there is a history in which God's grace is constantly being testified and mediated in different ways. What is given in this history again and again assumes a more profound meaning. The prophets are called and filled with God's Spirit in order to experience and express the faith of Israel more deeply and more fully, as Israel itself is called to express more deeply and more fully what is living in faith among the nations (who also have their prophets). Thus Jesus Christ is the one in whom the whole fullness of the Godhead lives and who for that reason assumes and expresses in the deepest way the blessing of men. God's Word, in which there is life for men, has become flesh in him.

Related to the history of salvation is the history of evil concerning Jesus. The geneological tree of Mathew 1 recalls the sins in his forefathers, but more clearly still, in all the gospels, Jesus encounters rebuffs among his people. He is as situated by the history of evil as he is by the history of salvation. Yet we do not recognize original sin in him, just as little as we do in Mary, and in fact we must say: still less than in Mary. That means that Jesus is not inwardly defined by the situation, that he is not subjected to sin, that sin has no power over him. While the Old Testament indicated in general terms the bond between the sins of the fathers and those of the children, the

New Testament speaks very definitely on the power and dominion of sin. It does so in contrast to Christ: death, the continuation of sin, reign until Christ (Roman 5, 14f.), through him we are redeemed from its dominion (Romans 6 and 7). This is possible, however, only because he himself is the totally free man, in whom the power of sin is present not to conquer but to be conquered (this, however, in human history, as we shall presently see). The immaculate conception of Mary is often contrasted with our orginal sin, understood as guilt. However, if one understands it as a situation that will lead to guilt (because it cannot lead to love), then such a situation would seem to be present in Mary, but not that power in it which urges to sin. The immaculate conception can also be understood as the grace which exercises its full power in the prevention of sin (1 John 3, 9). In both concepts it is clear that "immaculate conception" is realized in the highest way in Christ. If one looks only at the negative side of the prevention of sin, then the immaculate conception of Mary can be placed on a par with that of Christ. But this is a purely abstract view. If one concretely sees the salvific presence of God which prevents sin, then in Christ there is the fullness, in Mary the preparation and foreshadowing. This could lead to our seeing Mary's grace as a part of the history of salvation of Israel, as a last stage in the conquering of the power of sin within the chosen people of God, before he comes, in whom this power will be so conquered, that we can all resist it on the basis of his victory.

ON THE WAY AND AT THE SAME TIME COMPLETED?

Yet we have avoided saying that, in Jesus, sin *is* conquered from his first moment. Certainly, this is true, but it fails to emphasize the fact that it is conquered in human history. The fullness of the Godhead in Jesus Christ also has a history, precisely because it dwells there "bodily," humanly. Theoretically, such a history can be accepted by anyone who takes the term "one in substance with us" of Chalcedon seriously. But whoever assumes a pre-existent divine person in Jesus places this person outside his history, and to the degree that one sacrifices the human personhood of Jesus to his divine person, Jesus' history is robbed of its actual source,

117

the personal decisions of the man. Moreover, in "essentialistic" thought as borrowed from Greek philosophy, history is always conceived of as an accidental happening, which leaves the substance untouched by both things and persons. Thus scholastic theology neglects a number of soteriological differences, such as that between the Old and the New Testament. In christology there is a neglect of growth during Jesus' earthly life, especially a growth in knowledge, and of the fundamental difference between the earthly and the glorified life. We shall later discuss Jesus' growth in knowledge and the history of his decisions, but for the moment we shall confine ourselves to a few remarks on his earthly life and glorification.

The difference between Jesus' earthly and glorified life is not so much denied as minimalized by the scholastic thesis that Christ, during his earthly life, was *"viator simul et comprehensor,"* earthly pilgrim and possessor of the heavenly vision.[39] As we do not here wish to go into the arguments in favor of the heavenly vision of the earthly Christ, a more formal treatment of the thesis will now be presented. Yet this too seems an effective means of demonstrating its untenability, for if the thesis is held without closer definition, then it is a contradiction. One cannot be at the same time completed and on the way to completion, for the two are mutually exclusive. At least, they cannot be accomplished in the same way. For that reason, upholders of this thesis have viewed Jesus' being-on-the-way as on separate layer of being from his heavenly completion. This is particularly clear in their theory concerning Jesus' knowledge. For they are compelled to divide Christ's human knowledge during his earthly life into at least two layers: the *"scientia beata"* and the *"scientia experimentalis"* (and they even place between these another, intermediate layer, that of the *"scientia infusa"*). In the scholastic theory these two have clearly opposed characteristics: the *scientia beata,* the knowledge of the beatifying vision, includes an all-embracing knowledge, while the *scientia experimentalis,* on the other hand, is limited and capable of increase. This division of Christ's human knowledge has numerous drawbacks and actually increases the difficulties which arise against

39. St. Thomas, *Summa theol.* III, q. 9, a. 2. The various "layers" of Christ's knowledge are dealt with in qq. 9–12.

the two-nature christology. For to the divine person who super-sedes the human person there is now added a human all-embrac-ing knowledge, and this makes the idea of a humanly growing knowledge rather difficult, to say the least. A parallel difficulty can arise concerning the will of Jesus. These difficulties are in one way even more acute than those of the two-nature pattern in itself. Whereas scholastic theology, certainly in Thomism, did not equip the divine person of the Word with a proper divine consciousness and freedom, so that there is at least no express conflict between divine and human knowledge and will, such a conflict was never-theless introduced in Christ's human knowledge and will. For it is inconceivable how these can exist in one human subject without their nullifying one another, or the subject breaking up into two layers of human consciousness. Even if, with modern theologians we eliminate omniscience from Christ's *scientia beata* and reduce it to consciousness of his divine person, our difficulty remains inso-far as this knowledge (and the will coupled with it) is upheld as a knowledge of the heavenly completion. (There are theolo-gians who do away with this too,[40] but in doing so they are giving up the '*simul comprehensor et viator*"). In this way the division of Christ's human life of consciousness and will into two layers—with all the absurdity already inherent in it—would seem to be an unsuccessful attempt to escape from the contradictions of the "*simul comprehensor et viator.*" We would do better to relinquish this view.

The arguments produced in favor of this position are of a spec-ulative nature. They can be reduced to an appeal to the dignity of Christ's person and to his mediatorship for all gifts of salva-tion. That Christ's person stands in a state of completion is true if we think that we must affirm this person as an eternal, divine person, although God's eternity is not identical with completion, as the latter presupposes a previous state of incompletion. The eternity of the divine person in his divine nature, however, by no means entails an eternity in the human nature of Christ, which would then be a completion. The radical distinction that Chalcedon made

40. Thus Karl Rahner in "Dogmatic Considerations on Knowledge and Self-Consciousness in Christ," in *Theological Investigations V,* Baltimore and Dublin, 1966.

between the natures, the "without change, without confusion," specifically opposes this view. In parenthesis, the same can be said of all the attempts to give Christ's human operations and attitudes during his earthly life a transcendence above time and history, or a "perennial moment," as is done by those who wished to give a systematic-theological basis to the mystery doctrine of Odo Casel.[41] Consequently, an appeal to Christ's divine person seems to offer no ontological grounds for attributing to him a beatifying completion or an exemption from time in his human nature. An appeal to the dignity of the person has, as long as it does not have an ontological foundation, still less value. This holds for all arguments of convenience appealing to a *"decet"* (it suits). What do we know of what it suits God to do in his plan of salvation, unless it is from what God really does for us? Here we may bear in mind that the argument from the divine person formerly also led to a denial of the actual reality of Christ's suffering in so-called aphtharto-Docetism. How much less can one assume a completion or eternity in Christ's earthly human life if one bears his human person in mind and sees an eternal divine person as possible only insofar as this does not stand in the way of the human person. Precisely then, Jesus' completion during his earthly life, indeed from his human origin, becomes the more improbable, insofar as self-development in history is considered more essential for the human person.

A second argument refers to Christ's mediatorship.[42] He is mediator of all gifts of salvation, thus also of that of completion. This grace too we receive from his fullness. This means that he himself also possesses it. This argument is the only valid one, but it still says nothing of Christ's completion during his earthly life. For it is possible that only in his own glorified life is Christ the mediator of our blessed completion. Indeed, this *must* be so, since only as the Glorified he is the actual mediator, even of our earthly gifts of salvation: in his completion he has become source of eternal salvation to all who obey him (Hebrews 5, 9), in his glorification he causes the Spirit to come to us (John 7, 39; 16,

41. Thus L. Monden, *Het Misoffer als Mysterie,* Roermond, 1948, pp. 117f.

42. On this argument see E. Schillebeeckx, *Bewustzijnsleven* (note 14), pp. 237f.

7). Such a biblical outlook on the mediatorship of precisely the glorified Christ is probably the strongest counter-argument to the *"viator simul et comprehensor."* For it allows us to see a thought process in the New Testament which sharply distinguishes between the earthly and the glorified life of Christ, not only as humiliation and exaltation (Philippians 2, 6–11), but up to and including Christ's activity for our salvation. Johannine christology seems opposed to this view, however, insofar as in the fourth gospel Jesus is already in this earthly life making such self-pronouncements as that he will be the one to raise the dead, or that he is the way, the truth, the life and resurrection, or the good shepherd, or the true vine. But this agrees with the situation of the believers themselves, for whom already in this life faith means an eternal life, and unbelief judgment; it agrees, in short, with "realized eschatology." But that it is not intended to remove the contrast between the earthly and the glorified life of Christ is apparent not only from the above, whereby the sending of the Spirit is related to Christ's glorification, but also with the "form of a servant" which he assumes during the Last Supper (John 13, 3–15), and with Jesus' own obvious joy because he is going to the Father (John 14, 28). St. John's gospel gives no inducement to an ontological *"viator simul et comprehensor,"* and neither does the rest of the New Testament.

We should like to go further. The New Testament suggests for us a christological pattern which is precisely opposed to the above scholastic concept. It is the already mentioned adoption christology. This is a very ancient interpretation of Jesus' person, in which the messianic titles are attributed to him only on his resurrection or ascension: then he becomes Lord and Messiah (Acts 2, 36; Romans 10, 9; Philippians 2, 9), only then fully High Priest (Hebrews 1, 3f.; 5, 9f.), or even Son (Acts 13, 33; Romans 1, 4; Hebrews 1, 5). Here we stand at the other extreme from the being-*comprehensor* during Christ's earthly life. With the development of christology the adoption moves to Jesus' earthly life until it coincides with Jesus' origin and becomes incarnation. Previously, however, Jesus' sonship was attached to his baptism. The Father says to Jesus (Mark 1, 11 and Luke 3, 22 give the words in the second person): "Thou art my beloved son, with thee I am well pleased," and Jesus

121

sees the Spirit descending on him and according to John (1, 32f.) this Spirit remains in him. Even in a redaction of the gospels which includes an incarnation christology in its prologue—in John on the basis of the pre-existence, in Matthew and Luke on the basis of the conception from the Holy Spirit—this outlook on Christ's baptism has remained intact. Especially in John is it noteworthy that the Spirit comes down and remains in him who is described first as God's Word become flesh and who repeatedly testifies of himself that he has come from the Father. In Luke the Spirit comes down in corporal form onto him who is conceived because the Holy Spirit descended on his mother. Luke also contains, in the history of the infancy, twice a formula which speaks of Jesus' growth (2, 40. 52). Certainly, no growth in the spirit (or Spirit) is mentioned, as Luke does for John the Baptist (1, 80). But there is nevertheless a growth of Jesus in wisdom. He is filled with it (2, 40) and increases in it (2, 52), which then precisely shows Christ as earthly *viator* with regard to an important gift of salvation, which Paul regards as gift of the Spirit (1 Corinthians 2, 7–16) and which he invokes for the faithful (Ephesians 1, 17; Colossians 1, 9). Moreover, Jesus increases in favor with God and with man (Luke 2, 52).

There is thus within the gospels no contradiction when he who through an incarnation has come to us from God has himself grown in his relation to God and in the gifts of God. Of course, the concurrence of incarnation christology and (a remainder of) adoption christology in the New Testament has not yet been elaborated in a theological synthesis. But precisely thereby it invites us all the more to wonder at the fullness of God which dwells completely in this Man, but so "bodily" that it grows with him. This means that this growth is one that conquers our misgrowth and matures constantly to a self-communication to all. If only now we could experience this increase in wisdom, this growth in the Spirit from whom he was received, this maturing in the sonship of the Only-Begotten. But as we have already shown at length, it belongs precisely to the historical situation of Jesus that he is to such a great degree inaccessible for history in our sense. Here modern christology arrives at a paradoxical situation: it is ready fully to acknowledge the individual history of Jesus, but the exact content of the history escapes it. Here too we are left with a figure. It is thus worth elaborating this history from the viewpoint of Jesus' knowledge and will.

Jesus' Earthly Knowledge

THE SCHOLASTIC THEORY

In the preceding section we have discussed how Jesus, according to the scholastic concept, in addition to *viator* is also *comprehensor*, precisely because he has the knowledge of the beatific vision. Here we came into contact with the presuppositions of the scholastic theory on Christ's earthly knowledge, and we must stop here for a moment. The best theological argument for a *visio beata* lies in Christ's mediatorship, but precisely in the exercise of this mediatorship itself the distinction between the earthly life and the glorification, as we have said, plays a decisive role. Only the glorified Christ mediates for us the gifts of glory. However, arguments of convenience also come to the fore, both for Christ's *visio beata* and for the perfection of his knowledge in general, a perfection which for scholastic theology consists in the fact that Jesus, as Gutwenger has said, not only knows everything but also knows everything in every possible way.[43] For that reason Christ's human cognitive faculty must, in scholastic theology, by virtue of the unity with the divine Word, have already reached its goal in the *visio beatifica,* it must have been fulfilled in all its receptivity by infused knowledge, the *scientia infusa,* and eventually also—last but not least—it must have the growing knowledge of experience, the *scientia experimentalis,* in order for the active faculty, the *intellectus agens,* not to remain inactive towards the sensorial factor. All this constantly presupposes that all striving and potentiality is completely fulfilled through the union with the divine person. Logically, then, any presence in history would have to be denied of Jesus, and as we have said, his suffering and death would also have to be made a pretence. If one does not accept this fact, then an inner core of Jesus remains free of this suffering, of the fear of it, of all the human risks. For that reason we think that we should be understanding the entire data of the New Testament better if we replace the divine person in Christ with God's total presence.

43. E. Gutwenger, *Bewusstsein und Wissen Christi,* Innsbruck, 1961, p. 137: "Scholastic theology is not content that the soul of Christ knows all, but will have it that it knows all in all ways."

Scholastic theology could uphold its image of Christ's earthly life more easily than we can because its anthropology was different from ours. In fact, even the metaphysics and the theory of knowledge are different, for we can place necessary question marks on the whole construction of an infused knowledge in Christ, just as well as in the "departed souls." Does not God become here the supplementer instead of the creative initiator of human knowledge? And is human sensorial knowledge so passive that it lets itself be supplemented by "infusion" of its end result into the human intellect? But let us confine ourselves to anthropology. The concept of man which lies at the foundation of the scholastic theory of Christ's knowledge, as Gutwenger and Rahner have rightly pointed out, is most profoundly Hellenistic, and indeed on two counts.[44] First of all, it gauges the perfection of the man according to his knowledge, more particularly according to his clear insight, his vision. And further it sees history as only extrinsic and adventitious in human existence, it does not see it as an existence of self-development. Should the latter indeed be the case, then a lack of knowledge, especially of knowledge of the future, is not merely a lack, but at the same time it gives room for a freedom which itself makes the future. For man the lack of the (abstract) good of complete knowledge is the wherewithal for the higher good of venturing one's own future and thus of forming oneself from out of oneself and in oneself and in one's relation to others and the world. For Jesus it was good not to know the day which is his day and, as we may presuppose, not to have the issue of his mission present in his knowledge if he really wished to accomplish the mission himself. This also implies that he only slowly comes to a clear knowledge of this mission, and thus of his whole person and life's task. The whole scale of implicit consciousness, of questions, provisional interpretations and decisions, and of clear insights is to be expected in him. This is at least an anthropology which stands more open to an understanding of his appearance on earth than the thesis that he was always in all ways perfect in knowledge.

44. Gutwenger, *op. cit.* (note 43); K. Rahner, *op. cit.* (note 40).

THEOLOGICAL ARGUMENTS IN FAVOR
OF JESUS' HEAVENLY VISION

Theological arguments for a *scientia visionis* of Jesus during his earthly life are already refuted in what we have just said on his knowledge in general, and in the preceding section on his status of *comprehensor*. Theological development in this regard has been slowed down by the attitude of the teaching authority, although this has not expressed itself in a definitive way, nor by a definite rejection of the opposite opinion. There exists a letter of Pope Vigilius of 553, in connection with the second Council of Constantinople, which rejects ignorance in Christ as man (DS 419), but connects it with the Nestorian dual personality. Much more clearly opposed to such an ignorance is the decree *Lamentabili* (1907), in which those modernist theses are rejected which deny, besides unlimited knowledge, knowledge of the parousia and an ever-present messianic awareness in Jesus (DS 3428, 3432–35). More generally, and for our purpose more important, are a decree of the Holy Office of 1918 and a sentence from the encyclical *Mystici corporis* of 1943. The Holy Office makes note of three attitudes that cannot be safely taught, namely, that in Christ during his earthly life there was no visio beatifica, that he did not from the beginning know everything in the Word, that an assumption of limited knowledge in Christ has the same right as the thesis of his total knowledge (DS 3645–47). It is thus safe to assume the *visio* and thus an unlimited knowledge. Finally, the encyclical *Mystici corporis* appeals to this knowledge in order to say that Christ, during all his earthly life, loved the members of his mystical body with a salvific love (DS 3812). The encyclical *Haurietis aquas* of 1956 speaks in the same way, but only incidentally (article 328).

All of these pronouncements are made within the two-nature scheme, and if we are justified in placing this scheme in doubt, then these pronouncements must obviously be subjected to a different interpretation. But already the level on which, and the wording in which, they are given demonstrate that the theologian can suggest other interpretations. The pronouncement of Pope Vigilius leaves room for ignorance in Christ's human nature, if no Nestorian image

125

of Christ is connected with it. The modernist theses are rejected in *Lamentabili,* but without distinct censure (DS 3644), and in the pronouncement of the Holy Office they are "unsafe doctrine." But it remains fully possible for a theory which was rejected *in globo* as unsafe in 1907 and in 1918, now, in the 1970's, to be cleared of its dangerous implications. That this is truly possible is clear from the fact that the thesis of Christ's *scientia beata* on earth is today considerably modified by important theologians without protest from the magisterium. The words from *Mystici corporis* and *Haurietis aquas* on the knowledge and love of Christ for his own can, in such a modification, continue to keep their validity for the *glorified* Saviour.[45]

It may well be partly owing to the influence of these and similar magisterial pronouncements that the thesis of Christ's *scientia beata* has been upheld for so long. It has, however, as we have already said, been modified in two ways, which both clearly emerge in Rahner. The *scientia beata* is not conceived primarily as vision of an object, but as the consciousness that Jesus has of his own divine being-person. Thus it need not expressly occupy the consciousness of Jesus and fill it with an explicit content of knowledge. Consequently, it is conceived as an immediate vision, or rather as an immediate consciousness, but not as a beatific completion—*immediata* but not *beatifica.* In this way it can also be coupled with fear and suffering, and it will in fact intensify Jesus' suffering for sin. Thus the name *"visio"* or *"scientia visionis"* is retained, but it has become a human self-consciousness of Jesus, also as divine person, as eternal Son of God, from which the omniscience and the completion, that is, the status of *comprehensor,* have disappeared. One can wonder whether in such a concept the divine person can indeed be humanly conscious, in view of the difference of the natures. But in any case this reduction of the *visio* to the self-consciousness of Jesus fits best in our christology of the presence of God. The peculiar nature of Jesus' self-consciousness is thus that he knows God to be fully present in himself, that the Father is in him and he in the Father. Thus we are again confronted by the fact that Jesus' ego is conscious of itself in

45. Through this the Sacred Heart devotion would become less particularistic (and "doloristic") and would insert itself in the whole range of personal contacts of the Church with her now living Lord.

dialogue with the Father. In every man the inalienable ego comes to self-possession and self-expression in contact with the world, in dialogue with one's fellow men, and in all this in a self-orientation to God. This is no different in Jesus. The only difference—in which, as we have already said, all his human transcendence lies—is that the immediacy of his contact with God is predominant. From this viewpoint he interprets the world and in it he proclaims the kingdom of God. But on the other hand his self-consciousness as Son towards the Father is totally inserted in his contact with the world and his fellow men. Here alone does the peculiar ego-awareness of Jesus, inalienably and eternally peculiar only to him, as with the ego-awareness of anyone else, have content and become a consciousness of his mission.

JESUS' KNOWLEDGE OF HIS FUTURE

Jesus' consciousness of himself and of his mission is thus imbedded in all of his knowledge. The conviction of various theologians that this knowledge is all-embracing, according to which Jesus would be the greatest philosopher, poet, politician, and so forth of all time, has long given way to a real conception of Jesus' knowledge from experience, in which knowledge he not only (as Thomas thought) looked at things, but also and above all learned from men, from his people.[46] It is thus to be expected that he was in many ways dependent on the common concepts and outlooks of his contemporaries and countrymen. Exegetes are today coming into fruitful discussion with theologians and broadly affirm this point of view.[47] There is no mention anywhere in the evangelical tradition of an extraordinary knowledge of ordinary things from Jesus' environment. When in Luke 13, 1 a crime of Pilate is narrated to Jesus, there is nothing to indicate that this is not news to him; neither is Jesus' reaction a further explanation of the fact as such, but an inclusion of it into his call to conversion. Further, in his parables he does not impart any new knowledge on fishing and agriculture, but in every-

---

46. Thomas, *Summa theol.*, III, q. 12, a. 3.
47. R. E. Brown, *Jesus, God and Man, Modern Biblical Reflections*, Milwaukee, 1967, pp. 39–59 (Sections from the chapter "How Much Did Jesus Know?" of which we make use in the above).

thing that he encounters he finds a reference to the one thing that inspires him: the kingdom of God. In this context it is not surprising if Jesus quickly and fully saw through the reactions of the human heart to the message of the kingdom. The gospels also ascribe to him a knowledge of hearts, a penetration to the attitudes of persons. This is most explicitly the case with John, who also gives Jesus the most distinct self-pronouncements: thus that even this insight of Jesus becomes a knowledge of hidden events (John 1, 48; 4, 17; 6, 61; 16, 19). In general, however, such knowledge remains in John limited to an insight into hearts (2, 24f.; 4, 48; 5, 14), and this is even more the case in the synoptics (Mark 8, 37 and par.; 10, 21 and par.; 10, 38 and par.). It is possible that the predictions of Peter's denial and Judas' betrayal refer back to such a knowledge of hearts, through which Jesus had a presentiment, and that they were later filled out in more detail by the evangelists.

In general, something similar is most obvious in Jesus' predictions of the future. As concerns the near future, there are his predictions concerning his suffering, death and resurrection, and concerning the fall of Jerusalem. But the gospels were all written after Jesus' resurrection and, except for that of Mark, also after the fall of Jerusalem. By virtue of their whole manner of origin it is obvious that the text of Jesus' words on his own fate and that of the Jewish capital is defined on the basis of the events themselves.

For predictions of his passion this becomes probable through the fact that the three detailed predictions in the synoptics (Mark 8, 31 and par.; 9, 31 and par.; 10, 33 and par.) nowhere appear to be understood in their details by the disciples, and that precisely the Johannine predictions of Jesus' fate (John 3, 19; 8, 28; 13, 32) are seen by the evangelist as a prediction of the death on the cross (John 18, 32), while the wording itself goes no farther than a vague indication of a "lifting up" or "glorification," which could have been borrowed from Isaiah 52, 13. This does not mean that Jesus said nothing about his future suffering. On the contrary, the evangelists add further details to his words, the Synoptics in the text itself, John afterwards, probably with the precise aim of showing that Jesus had indeed spoken beforehand on his future fate; and the synoptics even give some detailed words in which Jesus speaks of his death (Mark 2, 20; Luke 13, 33). The most probable conclusion, then, is that Jesus saw this death coming, but did not possess any detailed foreknowledge of it. He saw it coming, because he possessed the same clarity concerning his own situation as concerning those of others. Whoever wishes to speak of a miracle here may rightly see this in the courage with which he was able to see his fate and accept it by remaining faithful to his mission, his task of proclaiming the kingdom of God.

In this attitude Jesus perseveres on the Mount of Olives and on the cross. He continues to place his trust in God's victory in him. The same can be said for the predictions concerning his resurrection as for his predictions concerning his suffering. Here particularly the disciples, according to the whole evangelical tradition, appear not to have understood (see in particular Luke 24, 19–26). In the words of Jesus to the High Priest, according to the synoptics, the fact that the Son of man resides at the right hand of the power of God is the answer to his death (Mark 14, 62 and par.), and in John, Jesus promises his return (14, 3. 19. 28; 16, 16) and the coming of the Spirit (in particular 16, 7). Thus there was probably more variation or more indefiniteness in Jesus' prediction of God's victory in him than is given by the concept of "resurrection" in itself. But that he was convinced of such a victory is undeniable.

The second point of Jesus' prediction concerning the near future is the fall of Jerusalem, which stands in the synoptic gospels in close connection with the parousia. In Jesus' so-called apocalyptic speech (Mark 13 and par.) it is difficult to separate the two subjects. Moreover, it is especially difficult here to make out which words refer to Jesus himself. If this is the case with Mark 13, 14–20, then here especially is there a warning which echoes the visions of Daniel (9, 27 and 12, 1). In Matthew the parallel text is somewhat more elaborated, though in Luke we hear Jeremiah (25, 13) and Zechariah (12, 3) in place of Daniel. It is obvious that Jesus had a presentiment concerning the fate of Jerusalem (according to Flavius Josephus' *Bellum Judaicum*, VI 6, 3 he was not the only one either), and that he spoke to its inhabitants warningly in great prophetic emotion (Matthew 23, 37–39; Luke 13, 34f.; 19, 41–44). He predicted its downfall at short term. It is even possible that the texts which proclaim the fulfillment of "all these things" within "this

129

generation" (Mark 13, 30) do not in fact refer to the just-mentioned coming of the Son of man, but to the fall of Jerusalem. Perhaps also the other "term text" (Mark 9, 1) would fall into such a context, while the expectation of the parousia during the preaching of the disciples in Galilee (Matthew 10, 23) is rather a pronouncement based on the situation of the community. A. Vögtle could be correct in ascribing the "*Naherwartung*" to the Palestinian community.[48] Perhaps the formula of Mark 9, 1, "there are some standing here," already expresses the question of the first believers concerning the relation between those who are living when the parousia happens and those who will have already died (see 1 Thessalonians 4, 15–17; 1 Corinthians 15, 51). In any case, the most certain point we can proceed from concerning Jesus' knowledge of the parousia is the text on his ignorance in Mark 13, 32 (and Matthew 24, 36): "Of that day or that hour no one knows, not even the angels in heaven, nor the Son, but only the Father." But this text does not in itself exclude all "*Naherwartung*" in Jesus himself. It remains possible that he only later arrived at this view. Moreover, it is possible, according to R. E. Brown, and even probable, that Jesus in this non-knowing did not correct the current concept of his contemporaries and in his pronouncements automatically used their language. In any case, it is very difficult to assume that he expressly left open an undefined period between his death and his return; otherwise the absence of the parousia would not have caused such a crisis in the communities (see 2 Peter 3).[49] On this point, too, Jesus does not speak to us primarily on the basis of a distinct foreknowledge, but on that of a trusting certainty concerning the victory of God and of God's kingdom.

JESUS' CONSCIOUSNESS OF HIMSELF AND HIS MISSION

The knowledge in which Jesus' consciousness of himself and his mission lies imbedded is thus to a great degree defined by his knowledge of his environment. Thereby Jesus understood events,

---

48. A. Vögtle, "Exegetische Erwägungen über das Wissen und Selbstbewusstsein Jesu," in *Gott im Welt, Festgabe Karl Rahner I:* Freiburg, 1964, pp. 608–667.

49. Brown, *op. cit.* (note 47), p. 78.

and therefrom too he learned the scriptures to which he was to refer. Therefrom as well does Jesus derive various religious concepts without correcting them, such as those regarding the devils and the punishment of sin. Precisely with and in all this material of concepts he proclaims God's kingdom (the latter expression also is historically defined). It could scarcely be otherwise if he was to express his own person and mission, and become conscious of them, in these concepts. Two things become understandable from this presupposition: that it was difficult for Jesus to express his consciousness in a title, and that this consciousness did not contain any previously outlined program.

The title of "Messiah" has, in the Greek translation "Christ," become a second proper name of Jesus. It is all the more remarkable that this title played only a very limited role during his earthly life. It is quite certain that Jesus was confronted with this title, even that he himself provoked the question of whether he was the Messiah. But he never appropriated this title without reserve. Further, he forbade his disciples to say that he was the Christ, he expressed himself towards the high priest, even after the confession of Peter, in terms of "Son of man," and on the latter occasion he predicted his suffering, which for the Jews of his time, Peter included, was indeed very unmessianic. We can then presuppose that he recognized himself much more in the picture of Yahweh's Servant from Deutero-Isaiah, but there are no texts making it indisputable that Jesus adapted this title to himself. The title of "Son of man," however, directly proceeds from Jesus, certainly in the eschatological Son of man pronouncements, but again it is not clear whether he meant himself thereby or another, or perhaps intentionally left this matter unresolved.[50] Also, words concerning "the Son," which are most likely to apply to Jesus himself, do not say explicitly that he himself is this Son, although they certainly suggest it.

This brief survey shows us that different reasons were possible why Jesus did not clearly express his self-consciousness by acknowledging for himself a predicate taken from the Old Testament or Judaism. These reasons can have existed as much in the predicates themselves as in the consciousness of Jesus. Certainly, Jesus' reticence

50. Bornkamm, *op. cit.* (note 29), chapter on "Jesus the Messiah"; Fuller, *op. cit.* (note 1), pp. 119–125.

concerning the title of "Messiah" is fully understandable. It was not then subject to the reinterpretation which it underwent through its application to the *resurrected* Jesus. During the earthly life of Jesus this title could, it is true, just as in the centuries before his life, have besides a warlike meaning (as in the so-called Psalms of Solomon) also a peaceful one (as in Zechariah 9, 9f.), but it remained a political predicate. The Messiah had to be a king in the literal sense of the word and the evangelical tradition is unanimous in that Jesus declined to fulfill this precise role, and even renounced earthly power and influence through sensational miracles (Mark 6, 45f. and par.; see John 6, 15; Mark 8, 11 and par.; John 7, 1–73; Matthew 4, 1–11 and par.). Here in a certain sense, then, the title means too little for Jesus. We can imagine that the image of the Ebed Yahweh inspired him more and this appears possible from the words at the Last Supper, without our being able to make out whether Jesus clearly had this image in mind. It is quite certain that the people saw him as a prophet (Mark 6, 14 and par.; 8, 28 and par.; Luke 7, 16), and that he himself understood his mission as such (Luke 13, 33; Matthew 13, 57). Concerning the title of "Son of Man," if it is true that practically only the eschatological pronouncements of the Son of man are of Jesus and that therein, just as in the words on "the Son," he does not expressly mean himself thereby, then the latter can have a double reason. It is possible that Jesus did not wish to surprise his listeners with the obligation to express themselves concerning his person. It is also possible that he himself was not yet so clearly conscious of his mission and person that he could express them in such an exalted title.

Both reasons for Jesus' reserve in assuming the most profound salvific titles, such as "Son of Man" and "the Son," directly and distinctly for himself become very probable if we now consider his mission. It is not the revelation of himself which is his task, but the proclamation of the kingdom of God. It is not he himself who is the center here: "Why do you call me good? No one is good but God alone" (Mark 10, 18 and par.); "To sit at my right hand or at my left is not mine to grant" (Mark 10, 40 and par.). Nevertheless, Jesus does have a completely individual place in the proclamation and offer of this kingdom, and this does not remain hidden in his attitude and words. He makes a clear distinction between God's previous utterances and actions and that which is now happening in and through himself, and this distinction concerns both the actions and the words of as well as Jesus' own person. What now happens in him, prophets and righteous men have not seen, but the disciples certainly have: for that reason they are blessed (Matthew 13, 16f. and par.). Conversely, those who were able to experience the earlier kings and prophets will pass judgment on "this generation," for "something greater than Jonah is here . . . something greater than Solomon is here" (Matthew 12, 41–42). That is why Jesus can then also oppose his words to what "is told to the forefathers," which means: that which, in the time before him, God himself has said. Over against this he says six times in Matthew 5: "But I say to you." The consciousness of newness and transcendence is thus not limited in Jesus to what is happening in him and the message which he has to bring. He is also aware of being a person who has the power to speak God's word further, a competence characterized by the community and perhaps already by Jesus' contemporaries as authority or full power (ἐξουσία), an authority which is expressly called greater than that of the scribes (Mark 1, 22 and par.) and which in fact also clearly surpasses that of the prophets. This authority is certainly exercised by Jesus in his well-known phrase: "Amen, I say to you," whereby perhaps in this amen an answer may also be heard to what the Father charges him to say and do.[51] Thus it is already obvious that Jesus' consciousness of being Messiah or Son is to be sought particularly in the role which he acknowledges himself in the presentation of the kingdom of God, in the "exousia" with which he speaks and acts. Hence it is possible for him to be named "Messiah" and "Son of man," and "the Son." Whether he did so himself would appear to be of secondary importance; the Church rightly ascribed these titles to him when his "exousia" was affirmed in his glorification.

But if Jesus' consciousness of himself as Messiah and Son is included in the consciousness of his relation to the kingdom of God, then it can also, together with his views concerning this kingdom, have undergone a development and even change. We have pointed out in the foregoing the paradoxical situation which theology has

51. H. Schlier, art. "Ἀμήν," in *Theological Dictionary to the New Testament I,* Grand Rapids, 1965.

arrived at on this point: while it is ready to accept the possibility of an inner development during Jesus' earthly life, it finds no written material to give it content. Earlier the dogmaticists were opposed to a development in Jesus' knowledge, particularly in his consciousness of his mission, while the exegetes were inclined to accept it. Now the roles are reversed: for the dogmatists such a development is not only a possibility, but a necessity, if Christ is to have been a genuine man in earthly time and history. If one gives this postulate content, then the exegetes say that the gospels give us no support for biographical reconstructions.

For some exegetes Jesus' word on his non-knowledge of "that day" is certainly authentic, but the "term texts" are probably from the Palestinian community. One exegete has said that in his ignorance Jesus takes over the "near expectation" of his contemporaries. In the same sense it can now be pointed out that precisely if Jesus' self-consciousness was not focused on definitive titles, when it is even more obvious that this self-consciousness also evolved with the circumstances and Jesus' attitude to them. It is then indeed possible that Jesus only slowly came to the discovery that the kingdom of God would certainly not be realized during his earthly life and that he should consequently not bring it near for his people through his preaching alone, in view of the unbelief which he encountered. Then also his rejection and his death came into perspective. Whatever there is of Jesus' self-interpretation in the light of the Ebed Yahweh figure, he did in any case decide not on a political Messiah role, but on a task of proclamation which no other power but that of his message. A foreknowledge of his suffering and death need not be included here, and is not even necessarily given, if Jesus has understood himself at his baptism as Servant of Yahweh.[52]

Here it must be pointed out again that the self-comprehension of Jesus, so far as it is made known to us, always encounters us as assumed in his relation to the kingdom of God and to God himself as his Father. However, Jesus understands himself always in relation to God, as Servant, as the Sent, as Son. This meant that he live his life in surrender, obedience, and trust. Here is the place to ask the question of whether Jesus' attitude to God was one of faith. It is precisely through our acceptance of a limited and grow-

52. This against Cullmann, *op. cit.* (note 1).

ing knowledge in Jesus that an affirmative answer to this question becomes probable. Faith is, however, more than a determined manner of knowing, it is first of all a surrender. For that reason we shall now take up the question of Jesus' faith in the context of his will.

Jesus' Will in His Earthly Life

JESUS' OWN HUMAN DECISIONS

In the ideas on Jesus' will during his earthly life we encounter the same difficulties as were discussed concerning his knowledge: Jesus Christ is a divine person and he is *comprehensor*. The idea that a pre-existent divine person makes Jesus' human nature enhypostatic finds its full elaboration in the various opinions on Jesus' free will. It cannot be otherwise or it would detract from his will at least his earthly freedom of choice. In speaking thus, we are *not* using as our point of departure a competitive relationship between the human choice and God's will or rule in general. In our opinion, the disputes in which both these realities have to be brought to a "*concordia*," the "*de auxiliis*" disputes in particular, proceed from the wrong assumption that both lie on the same level and thus stand in a competitive relationship. But God realizes man as individual person in a constant creation and thus man's decisions of will as the individual decisions of man, as free choices which emanate from man himself. Between God and man there may be a union of wills, but this reality can in no way be called one person. On the contrary, such a relation between God and the free man can best be described as a dialogue between *two* persons: God realizes man as a freedom *towards* himself. This is, however, precisely *not* the case if a divine person were to have an anhypostatic human nature. Then this divine person himself is the subject of human will. Or conversely: then that will is the decision of the divine person himself. Then, however, this human will does not have the individual decision or the individual initiative that emanates from human freedom (under God's creative realization). In this sense, Pope Leo says in his letter to Flavian that "the flesh *executes* what is of the flesh" ("*carne exsequente quod carnis est,*" DS 294). In such an

135

execution, however, Jesus' human nature is certainly an "instrument" of the Word, but Jesus is not a human person with an individual human freedom, an individual human decision, an individual human initiative. The third Council of Constantinople speaks in the same sense of a human will in Christ which "is subjected to his divine and almighty will" (DS 556). For our purpose, however, if we wish to take the human person and the human freedom in Christ seriously, we shall have to consider a human will which subjects *itself* to the Father. For that reason—we repeat—we must interpret Constantinople III in the same way as we did Chalcedon, that is, by replacing the pattern of the divine person with two natures, and thus two wills and two operations, with that of God's complete presence in the human person Jesus Christ with his own human will and actions. Here we could repeat our expression of the enhypostasia of the Word in the man Jesus. In him and in his human decisions the Word of God is person and realizes itself more and more as person.

With this last sentence our position towards the status as *comprehensor* of the earthly Jesus is again brought into focus. On this point, too, the various objections proceeding from Jesus' human will are quite clear. The being-*comprehensor* denies the being-*viator* precisely on the level of the human will. It reduces the being-*viator* to a loose appendix in Christ's manhood. For if Jesus as man has already attained completion, then he is no longer a human person who develops himself in his decisions. He makes then at most a few more arrangements concerning the realization of an attitude which is a firm given for him from the outset; there can then be no question of genuine temptations. One can, of course, say that the temptations of Jesus, if he is in addition to *viator* also *comprehensor,* are merely external temptations. Although we shall later say more about the temptations, the question can already be asked whether external temptations are genuine temptations. In an analogous way we can reason from the basis of the completeness of Jesus' holiness, obedience, or love, which must concur with the being-*comprehensor.* If there is such a completion from the outset, then this renders his increase in favor with God and with man an illusion. Then the acts of Jesus' moral and religious life are merely greater and greater manifestations of a love which itself no longer grows. This would have to rest on a one-sided relation between inward and outward:

the inner completion produces ever more excellent external actions, but does not itself grow in the process. This is already in conflict with the scholastic idea that the *habitus* becomes more intense through the acts, and more so as the person is constructed in his own decisions. Thus there is every reason, on the basis of Jesus' will, not to declare him to have been a *comprehensor* in any way during his earthly life.

ORIENTED TO THE KINGDOM OF GOD

The negative position which we have just described now gives us room to discuss the will of Jesus in a positive way. We have already shown that his was a life of human decisions which were both answer and initiative. Thus Jesus is fully responsible and the one who answers to the Father. It is also clear that his decision-making power grows. That he is without sin does not mean that he should be without history or without growth. On the contrary, not only did he increase in wisdom and favor (Luke 2, 52), but he also learned obedience in suffering (Hebrews 5, 8). We have also seen how much Jesus is situated in history and himself makes history, for others and for himself. His answer to the Father is also an answer to the situation in which he lives: these all form the cup which the Father gives him to drink. And each new answer gives a turn to his life. From this point of view we can discuss two characteristics of Jesus' decisions: their provisional nature and their orientation to the kingdom of God.

We like to interpret Jesus' earthly life in the light of his death on the cross. Here particularly we are following in the tracks of Paul, who wished to bring to the Corinthians no other knowledge but that of Jesus Christ and his crucifixion (1 Corinthians 2, 2). The epistle to the Hebrews already has him pronounce on his entry "into the world" his readiness for a unique sacrifice of his body, through which we are sanctified (10, 5–10). In addition to these tendencies in the New Testament such an interpretation of Jesus' life is justified by the conviction that in one's death the basic tendency of his life most clearly emerges. But this does not allow us to forget that this basic tendency can express itself in this life through a succession of choices, in which later decisions take up again or correct the earlier ones. The epistle to the Hebrews rightly sees Jesus' life as intended by the Psalm verse "I delight to do thy will" (40, 8), and John has him say, "My food is to do the will of him who sent me, and to accomplish his work" (John 4, 34). But the will of the Father demands of him an answer to changing situations. Here we can repeat what we said earlier on the possibility and probability that Jesus' view on the kingdom of God and on his own place in it was subject to growth and change. This entails the possibility and probability of changing plans in Jesus' life.

Two texts reinforce this probability. The first is Luke 9, 51: "When the days drew near for him to be received up, he set his face to go to Jerusalem. And he sent messengers ahead of him." Luke, the historian, certainly has a strong inclination to divide his narrative into periods (a reason why in Acts he describes Christ's ascension and the descent of the Spirit as an event that forms the caesura between the history of Jesus and that of the Church); moreover, his gospel has Jerusalem as the end point, just as Acts has it as point of departure (Luke 24, 33. 49. 52; Acts 1, 4. 8. 12). This does not eliminate the fact that the verse quoted, which forms the beginning of the so-called Lucan journey narrative, emphasizes only what the other synoptics also pass on to us: that Jesus, after a period of preaching in Galilee, extended his field of work (see Mark 10, 1; Matthew 19, 1) and finally went to Jerusalem, which, according to a suggestion in Mark 11, 11, seemed to be new and unknown for Jesus. All the synoptics place this departure from Galilee in a period of crisis: Jesus reproaches the leaders of the people with their unbelief and predicts his own rejection and death. It is here a matter, then, of much more than an external extension of territory: Jesus consciously leads his mission to a completion of life and death and will finally undertake death. Yet this does not mean that this death is henceforth an unavoidable fate. The history around Jesus could also have been different, as we have earlier shown. This becomes most obvious from the second text to which we here wish to draw attention: the prayer on the Mount of Olives. The synoptics each offer the possibility that it could have been otherwise; most expressly in Mark: "Abba, Father, all things are possible to thee; remove this cup from me" (14, 36). Here too, then, there is a keeping open of the other possibility; it is a matter of the Father's will, preferably for life, but if necessary, for death.

We have just seen the maneuverability in Jesus' choices, but there was also a constant element: he chose for God and his kingdom. Here we could speak at once of Jesus' sanctity, obedience, love, and sinlessness. But before we go into this attitude in Jesus' choice, it is perhaps best to look for a moment at the choices themselves that he had to make. For one cannot avoid the impression that before choosing for God and kingdom, Jesus had a very profound insight that it was a matter of the kingdom of God. Before being the holy one of God, the just, the loving one to the utmost, he was the morally and religiously awakened man. This moral and religious awakening answers to the *integritas* or *immunitas a concupiscentia*, at least as Karl Rahner once described this.[53] Freedom from concupiscence is in Rahner's description not a sort of moral impossibility of sinning, but being placed before the central choice of the final aim or the kingdom of God, and thus being removed from peripheral choices which limit themselves to means *as* means and do not directly affect the attitude with regard to the aim. It is then not an impossibility to sin, but the impossibility to commit venial sins and —we add to this—to do merely peripheral good deeds. Now concerning Rahner's argument we leave two questions undiscussed: whether the way of choosing which he describes is indeed precisely contraposed to concupiscence, which is from sin and leads to sin; and further whether this way of being could be real in the beginning of the human race. In any case, it seems extremely real to us in Jesus during his earthly life.

This too of course with limitations. Jesus had been a child and as a child could not yet have had the moral maturity of an adult. Moreover, only with difficulty can we presuppose that, as a normal man, any choice of going right or left or eating this or that was for him expressly involved with the kingdom of heaven. But if we may suppose that any man saw the deepest values that are concerned with human choice, then it was he. This follows from the fact that the kingdom of God is the constant theme of his preaching. He could confront others so emphatically with the choice of accepting or rejecting the kingdom because he himself was confronting

53. Karl Rahner, "On the Theological Concept of Concupiscence," in *Theological Investigations I*, Baltimore and Dublin, 1966.

the choice. For that reason he urged to a decision: "You cannot serve God and mammon" (Matthew 6, 24). He placed care for the kingdom of God before all: "Seek first his kingdom and his righteousness, and all these things shall be yours as well" (Matthew 6, 33), and he could do this because he himself chose in the light of the kingdom. For that reason various choices fall away as unimportant for the task which he had, which was of the highest importance for mankind: "Man, who made me a judge or divider over you?" (Luke 12, 14). The watchfulness of the good servant, even the cunning of seeing his own interest with the unjust steward, is for Jesus not too unworthy an image for arousing our attention to this choice. He must himself have always confronted this most profound choice.

JESUS' SINLESSNESS

And he answered it positively. Thus we come to the sinlessness of Jesus, which especially for late scholastic christology posed a very difficult problem: the question of Christ's freedom during his earthly life. Before we go on, however, let us first make two remarks on such sinlessness itself. First, perhaps we should recall once again that Jesus' sinlessness is not objectifiable. It cannot be established, either by an historical investigation or by an assessment of given data. It neither is nor was possible to measure ascertainable deeds of Jesus against fixed norms, for the simple reason that human deeds can never be investigated down to the root which defines their value, and because norms always emerge in a given situation. Jesus' sinlessness could become clear only for those who understood the basic attitude of his person, that is, the disciples during the days "that the Lord Jesus went in and out among us" (Acts 1, 21) and in the confirmation of their understanding through Jesus' resurrection. For that reason Jesus' sinlessness is the content of faith, not only for us who perceive it as message but also for those who met him face to face, for they too recognized it only by opening themselves to his person in freedom.

A second observation is that Jesus' sinlessness can be expressed much more positively as righteousness, holiness, obedience, service, love. Thus it becomes much clearer how the disciples knew it by means of what emanated from Jesus' person. Thus we find it given a wide variety of names in the New Testament. The very writings in which his sinlessness is affirmed also speak very emphatically in positive terms. The epistle to the Hebrews with its "yet without sinning" (4, 15) expresses Christ's holiness in terms which are partly positive and partly negative, when it describes him as the High Priest who is "holy, blameless, unstained, separated from sinners, exalted above the heavens. He has no need, like those high priests, to offer sacrifices daily, first for his own sins" (7, 26f.). St. John's gospel not only makes Jesus say, "Which of you convicts me of sin?" (8, 46), but also has him testify that he does everything that pleases the Father (8, 29), that he knows him and keeps his word (8, 55). Doing the Father's will is the motive force in Jesus' life: "My food is to do the will of him who sent me, and to accomplish his work" (4, 34). These later documents merely emphasize this tradition which comes to us via the synoptic gospels, in which Jesus lives and dies without prayer for forgiveness but in unconditional surrender to the Father's will.

In the late scholastic problematic it was not simply a matter of the factual sinlessness (*impeccantia*) of Jesus. It had in the meantime become an impossibility to sin, an incapacity for sin (*impeccabilitas*). This incapacity makes it necessary that Jesus act upon a command of the Father, thus for example the command or the mission (ἐντολή, *mandatum*) to give his life (and to take it back) in John 10, 18. In this verse Jesus speaks expressly of his freedom, but is this a freedom to choose, to say yes or no to the command or mission? Command of the Father, incapacity for sin, and the freedom of Jesus are the three terms of the late scholastic problem. If they concurred, then how is their concurrence to be made comprehensible? There have been about twenty attempts at an answer, which can be reduced to three types, depending on how they deal with the command of the Father, Christ's incapacity for sin, or with his freedom. The discussion is complicated by the various answers to the false problem of whether God's rule and human freedom concur, but even without that it is involved enough. In the beginning of this section we laid the foundations for the answer which we shall now give. For we then eliminated the idea of a non-personal human nature of Christ or of his being *comprehensor* during his earthly life. The first would make Christ's humanity

141

merely instrumental and thus rob him of a genuine freedom of initiative. The second gives him a complete freedom, which is doubtless greater than the freedom of a mere *viator,* but on the other hand precisely lacks the possibility of saying yes or no, which takes away the possibility of merit.

This means that we must modify the second term of the problem. *Impeccabilitas* must be reduced again to *impeccantia.* This can concur with freedom of choice, which renders superfluous a further analysis of the mission or the command of the Father (such an analysis attempts indeed to apply juridical categories to the relation between God and man: a strict command, a strict command with possibility of dispensation, a non-strict command). This reduction appears to us fully justified. Scripture tells us that Jesus *did not sin,* but it does not say whether he *could* sin or not. By limiting oneself thus to factual sinlessness, one is doing no less than by ascribing to Jesus an essential incapacity for sin. He has then just as much conquered evil and rejected Satan and stands just as much before us as the High Priest who does not sacrifice for his own sins, the Redeemer who need not first be redeemed himself. With Mary's sinlessness too (freedom from personal sin is never mentioned officially by the magisterium) a qualitative difference remains, in view of the fact that it is not the *fullness* of God's presence which preserves her from sin. By speaking only of factual sinlessness in Christ one is elaborating the redemptive victory over sin which arose in him in a different but also in a better way, for it is a more human, more real way. An incapacity for sin would always have been determined before Jesus' human insertion of will; with such a course of affairs, however, his human will is not redemptive and our human will not redeemed. Jesus would then again stand outside history. In particular, we should then be doing wrong to what the New Testament tells us about his temptations.

JESUS' TEMPTATIONS

The Greek words πειράζειν and πειρασμός and the Hebrew words which they represent refer to more than what we call temptation or seduction. πειράζειν means: to try, to investigate, to examine, to put to the proof, to that extent it is roughly synonymous with δοκιμάζειν.

142

One can examine onself (1 Corinthians 11, 28; 2 Corinthians 13, 5), those who call themselves apostle (Revelations 2, 2) or the spirits (1 John 4, 1), even everything (1 Thessalonians 5, 21). Jesus has been put to the proof (as in Matthew 16, 1) and God can be put to the proof (as in Acts 15, 10). On the other hand, God tries man (1 Corinthians 10, 13; Hebrews 11, 17), but Satan does so too (1 Corinthians 7, 5). From all this it is obvious that such proofs can have a good or neutral meaning, but also a hostile one. It is to this latter meaning that πειράζειν develops, especially if it is exercised by Satan, and then it means: to fascinate, tempt, seduce. Mark says quite simply that Jesus during his forty days in the wilderness "was tempted by Satan" (1, 13) and Matthew (4, 1–11) and Luke (4, 1–13) describe the famous three temptations in the form of a dispute, in which the quotations from Deuteronomy and also the words "If you are the Son of God" refer to Israel's temptations in the wilderness. More still, the narration refers, whatever one may think of its literary forms and historical character, to Jesus' whole life on earth. Such a reference can be seen in the sequence of the temptations: in Matthew they end on a mountain, as does his gospel; in Luke they end in Jerusalem, as likewise does his gospel. Luke, moreover, makes reference to a later period, probably to Jesus' suffering, explicit through the closing phrase: "the devil . . . departed from him until an opportune time" (4, 13). But it is mainly Jesus' word (ὕπαγε, σατανᾶ), that reminds one of a word to Peter that seems to to Satan in the last temptation in Matthew, the "Be gone, Satan" be *ipsissima vox Jesu* (Mark 8, 33; Matthew 16, 23). Thus the scene in the wilderness opens up an outlook on the entire life of Jesus, and especially his suffering, as temptation.

The rebuke of Peter shows, moreover, together with the wilderness narrative, what the content of this temptation was: to choose the will of man oriented to success without suffering over the will of God, which demanded loyalty even unto suffering. In this light especially we can interpret Jesus' fear and prayer on the Mount of Olives as a temptation and victory. The same holds for Jesus' outlook on his suffering in John 12, 27–32. In all of these episodes Jesus considers the possibility of escape, and the more primitive the text, the more he prays for this possibility; but they all end with his surrender to the Father. John speaks here of trouble, Mark and

Matthew of distress, always with quotations from Psalm 41, 6f.; the latter use words which indicate intense fear and trembling (Mark 14, 33; Matthew 26, 37); Luke speaks of sweat like blood, and agony (22, 44f.). When Jesus incites his disciples to prayer, Mark and Matthew interpret this event as a temptation to themselves, while in Luke this event occurs at both the beginning and end of the narration. Jesus' words in Mark and Matthew: "the spirit indeed is willing, but the flesh is weak," can have been uttered from his own experience; but it is only John who sees it as a confrontation between Jesus and Satan: "The ruler of this world is coming. He has no power over me; but I do as the Father has commanded me, so that the world may know that I love the Father" (14, 30f.).

Everything here gathered from the gospels finds its extension and deepening in the epistle to the Hebrews.[54] This epistle is well known as the only New Testament document that consistently interprets Christ's act of redemption in a terminology of sacrifice and views him as the eternal High Priest. But the meaning of this sacral terminology must not be exaggerated; and in fact one can maintain that the terms "high priest" and "sacrifice" precisely in this epistle are desacralized in the most radical way. Jesus' sacrifice appears to be the sacrifice of himself and it is realized in the obedience and the surrender of the Ebed Yahweh. And this is carried out in trial, weakness, suffering, and thus in a growth to completion. We have already quoted from this epistle on the sanctity of the High Priest. But we also find: "For we have not a high priest who is unable to sympathize with our weaknesses, but one who in every respect has been tempted as we are, yet without sinning" ($\pi\epsilon\pi\epsilon\iota\rho\alpha\sigma\mu\acute{\epsilon}\nu\upsilon\nu$ $\delta\grave{\epsilon}$ $\kappa\alpha\tau\grave{\alpha}$ $\pi\acute{\alpha}\nu\tau\alpha$ $\kappa\alpha\theta'$ $\acute{o}\mu o\iota\acute{o}\tau\eta\tau\alpha$ $\chi\omega\rho\grave{\iota}\varsigma$ $\acute{\alpha}\mu\alpha\rho\tau\acute{\iota}\alpha\varsigma$: Hebrews 4, 15). This sentence contains the core of what the epistle to the Hebrews tells us of Jesus' temptations and trials. First of all, Jesus' capacity to sympathize with our weaknesses is noted, a characteristic which the writer wishes to see realized in every high priest. The high priest in general is "himself beset with weakness" (5, 2), but Jesus is just as much beset. He wished to share our existence which was subjected to death and the devil (2, 14f.). Not angels, but humans did he care for (2, 16): "Therefore he had to be made like his brethren

54. See Cullmann, op. cit. (note 1), in the chapter on Jesus as the High Priest.

in every respect, so that he might become a merciful and faithful high priest in the service of God, to make expiation for the sins of the people" (2, 17). Here too there is the phrase "in every respect" (κατὰ πάντα), just as in 4, 15: his equality with us is in every respect, in weakness, in trials and temptation; only in sin is it lacking.

This weakness causes Jesus to be tried by suffering: "For because he himself has suffered and been tempted, he is able to help those who are tempted" (2, 18). Jesus' weakness in this suffering is most vividly described in the fifth chapter, with words which show Christ's human-ness just as fully as the synoptic account of the Mount of Olives: "in the days of his mortal life he has with loud cries and tears (μετά κραυγῆς ἰσχυρᾶς καὶ δακρύων) offered up prayers and supplications to God who could save him from death. He is heard for the sake of his piety (ἀπὸ τῆς εὐλαβείας, which could also mean: from his fear: see the strengthening by the angel in Luke 22, 43); although God's Son, he learned obedience through what he suffered" (Hebrews 5, 8). All this weakness in suffering, ending in crying and weeping, allows the possibility that Jesus could refuse suffering. His sufferings, which "in every respect" are the same as ours, leave open then the possibility for refusal to sin, rather than exclude it from the outset. The learning of obedience also points in this direction.

We have dwelt so long on the New Testament testimony on Jesus' temptations because this leads to where Christ's personal and historical manhood would also lead us: he is sinless, not through an incapacity for sin which merely makes Christ's temptations external and their results decided in advance, but through the strengthening, the hearing of God which makes Jesus conquer the real possibility present in him to sin. This precisely makes Jesus' worthy of a divine sonship in humanity, and indeed in a becoming, developing humanity. The epistle to the Hebrews expresses this point by ending the above-quoted sentences with a thought on Jesus' *completion,* his progress to perfection: "And being made perfect he became the source of eternal salvation to all who obey him, being designated by God a high priest after the order of Melchizedek" (5, 9f.). This text gives the impression that Jesus' high priesthood is present only in his completion, just as this was said before of his divine sonship (5, 5f.; see Acts 13, 33; 2, 36). In any case, with the resurrection or glorification Jesus' high priesthood becomes completed, fruitful,

145

and powerful for others, as Paul also says of the sonship (Romans 1, 4). Here what we have often illustrated again comes to the fore: it is necessary to include adoption christology in incarnation chistology. Jesus' divine sonship is at the same time with his manhood a reality-in-becoming: the whole fullness of the Godhead takes possession of him more and more, by affirming Jesus in obedience and by making him conquer sin and Satan.

JESUS' FAITH

What we have said in the foregoing of Jesus' knowledge and will during his earthly life can now be concluded with a discussion of a possible *faith* within him. Believing is a deed or attitude of the whole person: it is not merely a recognition of truths, and it is just as little—which we from reaction are inclined to think at present—a blind surrender, resting on a purely subjective decision.[55] Because believing is not merely the recognition of truths which cannot be seen—*"fides est circa res non visas"*—it is not out of the question to ascribe faith to Jesus during his earthly life even if at the same time he is acknowledged the heavenly vision. But we do not need to go into this combination here, because we have excluded this vision itself for the earthly life. Thus we stand, more than does classical Catholic christology, open to the words of Hebrews 12, 1–3: "Therefore, since we are surrounded by so great a cloud of witnesses, let us also lay aside every weight and sin which clings so closely, and let us run with perseverance the race that is set before us, looking to Jesus the foundation and perfection of our faith, who for the joy that was set before him endured the cross, despising the shame, and is seated at the right hand of the throne of God. Consider him who endured from sinners such hostility against himself, so that you may not grow weary or faint-hearted." In the context quoted here the words "foundation and perfection of the faith" should apparently be actively understood, so that we see Jesus himself as the one who initiates the attitude of faith and who in the race of the faith reaches the good goal. However, we must consider that others give a different interpretation to these words, and especially that nowhere in the

55. As in the "non-cognitive blik conception of faith" in Paul van Buren's book (note 9).

New Testament is Jesus presented simply as a subject of faith. For that reason a closer reflection is demanded, which first of all raises the question of what scripture understands by believing and then whether such a faith can be ascribed to the earthly Jesus.

The first question can only be briefly answered here.[56] It is generally agreed that in scripture faith is an attitude of the whole person. The will, the surrender to and the leaning on God are there of more concern than is admitted in the analyses of the act of faith in later Catholic theology. In the concept of faith of the Old Testament this surrender to and this leaning on God are predominant; faith coincides with hope and also with obedience, as appears especially in the faith of Abraham. A confession of Yahweh's acts of salvation and of his oneness is, however, also present in the Old Testament, apart from the question of whether it comprises strict *formulas* of confession. In the New Testament, however, the confession comes to prevail more. For so far as the synoptic gospels refer us back to the earthly life of Jesus they show especially the faith that is hope, as this is demanded of those who wish to be healed or freed by Jesus. Mark has Jesus demand right at the beginning: "believe in the gospel" (1, 15). The recognition and confession of this gospel are further to characterize faith in the New Testament, while it never becomes merely intellectual but remains an answer of the whole man. In Acts faith sometimes directs itself to the name of Jesus (3, 6. 16), which takes on its meaning through the message concerning his resurrection. In Paul faith is the attitude of the man who accepts God's justification through Christ (Galatians 2, 16; 3, 6–26; Romans 3, 22–31; 4; 5, 1; 9, 30–33), but this faith is precisely for that reason also acceptance of the good news of Christ's death and resurrection (1 Corinthians 15, 1–11). We see that in Acts and in Paul "faith" ($\pi\iota\sigma\tau\iota\varsigma$) already takes on the objective meaning of: the message of faith, the content of faith (Acts 6, 7; 13, 8; Galatians 1, 23). In John eternal life is already on earth bound with believing, as in Paul righteousness (John 3, 16. 36; 5, 24–26;

56. With references to, *inter alia,* J. Alfaro, "Fides in terminologia biblica," in *Gregorianum* 42 (1961), 463–505; *idem,* "Foi et existence," in *Nouv. Revue Théol.* 90 (1968), 561–580; L. Malevez, "Foi existentielle et foi doctrinale," in *ibid.* pp. 137–154. More speculative are studies such as Jean Mouroux, *I Believe,* New York and London, 1959; August Brunner, *Glaube und Erkenntnis,* Munich, 1951.

6, 40. 47; 10, 27f.; 11, 25f.; 20, 31), but faith is at the same time the knowledge of Jesus as God's Son, sent precisely to bestow this life (John 8, 24; 10, 38; 17, 8. 21). The fruits of believing and the knowledge of faith therefore coincide: "This is eternal life, that they know thee the only true God, and Jesus Christ whom thou hast sent" (John 17, 3).

In the first epistle of Peter, however, faith is directed to the future resurrection. It is for that reason identified with hope (1, 21), while in Paul it is bound with hope but yet distinct from it (1 Thessalonians 1, 3; 1 Corinthians 13, 13). The epistle to the Hebrews, which we quoted above because the author seems to ascribe faith to Jesus himself, keeps close to this identification of faith and hope, at least in chapter 11. We can then regard the whole epistle as an incitement to hold fast to the faith. This stimulus is constantly expressed after a dogmatic passage: in 2, 1–4, after the introduction, in 3, 7—4, 13 after the comparison of Christ with the angels and with Moses, in 5, 11—6, 20 after the first presentation of Christ as high priest, and finally in the great closing passage 10, 19—13, 35 after the elaborate comparison of Christ's priesthood and sacrifice with the high priest and the conciliatory sacrifice in the Old Testament. Already through this connection with an elaborate, and even a "perfected" doctrine (6, 1) the content of faith is apparent: it is paying "attention to what we have heard" (2, 1) and "holding fast our confession" (4, 14). It is noteworthy, however, that the third incitement to faith (5, 11—6, 20) scarcely names the word "faith" itself, but speaks of the doctrine and of our hope. Both elements also recur in a chapter from the closing passage, which evokes the witnesses in faith of the Old Testament. This is the already mentioned chapter 11, which begins with a sort of definition of the faith: ἐστιν δε πίστις ἐλπιζομένων ὑπόστασις, πραγμάτων ἐλεγχος οὐ βλεπομένων. The Vulgate gives for ὑπόστασις: *substantia,* a translation which suggests something like "the foundation of what we hope" and in agreement with this: "the proof of the reality of invisible things." Another possibility is to understand the words ὑπόστασις and ἐλεγχος actively: "faith now is firm expectation of hoped for conviction of unseen things." The active meaning of ὑπόστασις is certainly possible and is also defended: in Hebrews 11, 1 it can perhaps still be suggested by the contrast with the ὑποστολή, the "faint-heartedness," the "shrinking back" of Hebrews 10, 39. In any case, the objective and the active concept of both key-words in Hebrews 11, 1 can be traced in the rest of this chapter, which is why it even remains possible for both meanings to be present in this verse itself. In the cloud of witnesses who live from the faith the connection of faith with hope and also with obedience appears obvious. Thus the epistle to the Hebrews tells us of all the riches of the New Testament concept of faith. It is no wonder that this document, which in its totality is such an urgent evocation to belief, also relates Jesus to our attitude of faith.

If we enquire now after the individual faith of Jesus,[57] after him as subject of faith, then we can cite many words in the gospels which ascribe to him an attitude of faith. The words which stimulate us to trusting and never-ceasing prayer must be an echo of Jesus' own prayer. In the preceding section we have shown that Jesus had no distinct foreknowledge of the final completion. He did, however, speak of it trustingly as of God's ultimate victory and redemption and could for that reason say that the present acceptance of the kingdom of God and of himself or even the glass of cold water given to one's neighbor will be rewarded at the judgment. Of his own fate, too, Jesus had no distinct foreknowledge, but he could look his death in the face and accept it with the certainty that his Father would conquer in him. His words before the Sanhedrin testify to this fact (Mark 14, 62). Matthew lets Jesus' enemies revile him on the cross with words which bear testimony to Jesus' believing trust: "He trusts in God; let God deliver him now, if he desires him" (Matthew 27, 43 = Psalm 22, 9). All the evangelists give words of Jesus on the cross which illustrate his trust in God; Mark and Matthew in the prayer of Psalm 22 (Mark 15, 34; Matthew 27, 46), Luke in Jesus' certainty concerning his entry into paradise (23, 43) and his prayer: "Father, into thy hands I commit my spirit" (23, 46 = Psalm 31, 6), John finally in the cry: "It is accomplished" (19, 30). Also and precisely in the abandonment the Father was for Jesus the goal, so that John can have him say before his suffering: "The hour is coming, indeed it has come, when you will be scattered,

---

57. On this subject see, *inter alia*, G. Ebeling, *Word and Faith*, New York, 1963; L. Malevez, "Le Christ et la foi," in *Nouv. Revue Théol.* 88 (1966), 1009–1043.

every man to his home, and will leave me alone; yet I am not alone, for the Father is with me" (16, 32). Does this not all justify the phrase in Hebrews 12, 2, that Jesus is "foundation and perfection of our faith"?

It must be pointed out here that the verb "to believe" ($\pi\iota\sigma\tau\epsilon\acute{u}\epsilon\iota\nu$) is nowhere directly applied to Jesus as subject. He is thus not classed with the believers, not placed on the same level with them, not even in the epistle to the Hebrews. One reason for this can lie in the connection made in all the New Testament between faith and kerygma. Christian faith is not merely a trusting surrender to God, it is specifically such a surrender which leans on what God does and is for us in Jesus Christ, and what is said and proclaimed to us concerning him. And it is precisely this specific element which is not present in Jesus' belief. On earth he could not believe in his resurrection as a fact, as we do now; he could only hope for it, and this probably only in his general trust in the Father's victory through him. Moreover, this redeeming fact could not be said and proclaimed to him from another, for it happened in himself. Of course, God's word came to Jesus during his earthly life through the scriptures, that is, through the Old Testament: he had to believe in God's salvific operations in Israel, and, moreover, in himself. But no Messiah was proclaimed to him, no redeemer to save him, for he himself was Messiah and redeemer and only-begotten Son. Here we touch again on the immediacy in the relation of Jesus to his Father. God has in him, in an eschatological, definitive, unsurpassable way, completed his salvific operations and made a new beginning; for that reason Jesus had to believe in God without attaching himself to a higher mediator. His faith was not faith in the proclamation of another Christ, it was not an attachment to anyone, but an—in this regard—unmediated surrender to God himself. In this immediacy it agrees with a *visio beatifica,* but it is distinguished from it through its earthly state.

This comparison between Jesus' faith and that of the Christians is nowhere made clear in the New Testament. Neither is it a direct theme in the conclusion of the epistle to the Hebrews, where we see him presented as "leader" of the faithful (12, 2). The "cloud of witnesses" (12, 1) that is presented in the eleventh chapter does not refer to the followers of Christ, but to the preceding Old Testament. To them can be applied what the epistle says further of Old Testament worship: that the Law has made nothing perfect (7, 19), that it was only a shadow of the good things to come (10, 1). For that reason all the believers from this "first testament" can be described as those who did not achieve perfection, at least not without us and without Christ: "And all these, though well attested by their faith, did not receive what was promised, since God had foreseen something better for us, that apart from us they should not be made perfect" (11, 39f.). Their faith did not see the perfection; we do see it, not in ourselves but in Christ. Against this background we can read the beginning of chapter 12 again: "Therefore, since we are surrounded by so great a cloud of witnesses, let us also lay aside every weight and sin which clings so closely, and let us run with perseverance the race that is set before us, looking to Jesus the foundation and perfection of our faith." The more objective words "foundation and perfection" are justified in this context, for *we* see in Christ the perfection and find in him the foundation, neither of which were yet present for the believers of the Old Testament. The question is, however, whether the epistle to the Hebrews does not say more when it calls Jesus τὸν τῆς πίστεως ἀρχηγὸν καὶ τελεωτήν. This already holds for the *hapax legomenon*, τελεωτής, and it certainly holds for ἀρχηγός.

The word "instigator" indicates someone who begins something, chronologically and also causally. Thus Jesus is named ἀρχηγός of life (Acts 3, 5: in opposition to the murderer Barabbas) and in the epistle to the Hebrews itself ἀρχηγὸν τῆς σωτηρίας (2, 10). Here Jesus is discussed as pioneer of salvation on his way to perfection through suffering. Precisely the same thought also follows in 12, 2: "For the joy that was set before him endured the cross, despising the shame, and is seated at the right hand of the throne of God. Consider him who endured from sinners such hostility against himself, so that you may not grow weary or faint-hearted." Precisely these latter phrases make it necessary to understand Jesus at least as much in the active sense as ἀρχηγὸς and τελεωτής of the faith. He was not merely foundation and perfection of it, but also beginner and perfecter, instigator and completer. The witnesses of faith in the Old Testament could not achieve the completion which they looked forward to in their own day; they can do so only now,

151

with us, because Jesus was the first to achieve this completion. Thus Jesus is, during his earthly life, primarily a believer in his own completion, the prophet of his own glorification, which completion and glorification mean salvation for us. If we have said that he did not need to hope for the salvation of any other, now it becomes even more clear that he had to hope for his completion and our salvation from God as brought about in him: completed by God he has become source of salvation for whoever obeys him (Hebrews 5, 10), doubtless primarily through believing in him.

These reflections from the New Testament and especially from the epistle to the Hebrews illustrate Jesus' completely unique place among believers. Perhaps, as we suspected, this uniqueness is the reason why there is no question simply of his faith. But precisely the words from the epistle to the Hebrews show that his attitude of faith is the same as ours, that he has gone our way of faith as example and pioneer. The surrender of faith remains in its completion, in Jesus and in us. But Jesus also went our way of faith-in-earthly-darkness and he cultivated hope and obedience among the contradictions of sinners and with loud cries and tears. His aversion and fear are, however, conquered by faith and alchemized to love for us. That was his earthly history. We shall now briefly discuss his completion.

Jesus' Heavenly Completion

The resurrection is not merely one of the events of Jesus' history, and our confession of the resurrection does not form merely one of the articles of faith. "If Christ has not been raised, your faith is futile and you are still in your sins" (1 Corinthians 15, 17): the resurrection and the glorification which began with it do not form an incidental reward or crowning of Christ's redemptive work, but are what it stands or falls by. For that reason, preaching without resurrection is without content and our faith without foundation or value (1 Corinthians 15, 14. 17). This also means that our christology proves its worth only through confessing resurrection and glorification in the correct way; then Jesus not merely *was* the one in whom God wished to be our salvation in fullness, but he *is* still. The christology which we have elaborated in the foregoing compels us more particularly to present Christ's resurrection and glorification as real. If one qualifies Christ's person as divine, there is the temptation to regard him in his glory after his earthly life merely as God, just as in the pre-existence before it. His glory becomes, then, the absence of the assumed human nature. It is true that this is only sporadically asserted at the dogmatic level as having effect after Christ's parousia, but in the practical experience of many Christians the Lord has at least in his ascension put away his humanity. In the christological pattern of this book nothing would then remain of Jesus with certainty. This is a challenge to confess and describe the resurrected and glorified man Jesus as real for us now.

NOT OBJECTIFIABLE

Reality is always considered on the basis of what is ascertainable, objectifiable. For that reason we must from the outset irrevocably stand by two things: Jesus died our death, and in his resurrected life he is accessible only for faith.

Jesus died our death, without return. Hence the oldest kerygma also narrates his burial (1 Corinthians 15, 4). Two evangelists find it important to narrate the fact that this death was officially ascertained (Mark 15, 44; John 29, 33). Jesus is awakened not only from the grave, but from the kingdom of the dead, or, in a Hebraicism: from the dead (1 Corinthians 15, 12; Romans 6, 9; Acts 2, 24. 31; 3, 15; 4, 10; 10, 41; 3, 30). This has then also become the formula of the Apostolic confession of faith; the words "he descended into hell" say in the first instance (thus apart from the relevant salvific meaning of Christ for the fathers, which was later seen in it) the same in the opposite direction. Jesus really died. He entered the kingdom of the dead, the "*sheol*" of the Psalms, from whence there is no return to our earth. His death is then also a dying "once for all" (Romans 6, 10). Thus his resurrection is precisely the opposite of the awakening of the dead, described in the gospels and elsewhere, or of medical reanimations. Christ does not return to this earthly life, but crosses the gateway of death to the other life, the life of completion. He is the "first fruits of those who have fallen asleep" (1 Corinthians 15, 20), the "first-born from the dead" (Colossians 1, 18) or "of the dead" (Revelations 1, 5). For that reason he is the first to arise, and those who belong to him follow on his coming. His resurrection is not a return to this life, but a preceding into the completed, ultimate, eternal life.

This life is that of "heaven." Christ has not only arisen, but also "ascended into heaven." We shall be discussing the relation between resurrection and ascension shortly, but for the moment it is sufficient to say that since this ascension Christ's life is heavenly. In spite of the spatial expressions of scripture (Acts 1, 9); Ephesians 4, 8–10), no one today would think situating this heaven in some section of our material universe. Nor is heaven further off still; it belongs to another dimension, it is not a place but a way of being. It is the completed way of being, completed to good, completed in God, for "heaven" means in scripture first of all the firmament and then the throne room of God above that firmament. Christ is dead once for all, but he lives to God (Romans 6, 10). Indeed, he is sitting at the right hand of God the Father. The words of Psalm 110, 1, according to the Septuagint: "The Lord says to my lord: Sit at my right hand, till I make your enemies your footstool," is in the New Testament abundantly adapted to Jesus (Mark 12, 6 and par.; Acts 2, 34f.; Hebrews 1, 13; 10, 12f.; 1 Peter 3, 22).

Sitting beside God is a sharing in his rule, and this again directs our attention to earth. The heaven of Jesus is not only not a place outside our earth, neither is it a way of being which withdraws him from the earth. Jesus is on the contrary now in and from heaven, Lord over his community and over God's world, until on the parousia his enemies are destroyed to the last man (1 Corinthians 15, 25). It is true that in the New Testament there is still a trace of the idea that heaven has withdrawn Jesus from earth until his return (Acts 1, 9–11), but the belief that he already prevails now, present and active, has, partly through the adaptation of Psalm 110, 1, become predominant. It is countered by the experience of the presence of the Holy Spirit, but this Spirit comes from the exalted Christ (Acts 2, 33; John 16, 17), and both are even identified (2 Corinthians 3, 17). Thus Christ's being in heaven is obviously identical with his salvific power on earth. The gospel of St. Matthew has in place of an ascension these words of the resurrected Christ as its conclusion: "All authority in heaven and on earth has been given to me. . . . Lo, I am with you always, to the close of the age" (28, 18. 20).

Insofar as Jesus' life is completed and celestial, it is removed from the needs of this earthly existence. The recalled Lazarus had to be unbound (John 11, 44), but the resurrected Christ is present in spite of closed doors (John 20, 19. 26). The daughter of Jairus had to be given food (Mark 5, 43), but whoever literally takes the meals of the resurrected Lord (for example, Luke 24, 41–44) continues to deny that he was subjected to hunger. And not only are our earthly needs foreign to him; but also the imperfect, the impersonal, that is always present in our human communication on earth seems to have been removed from him. This now is precisely the ascertainability of things, their objectifiability, to which we, through our earthly corporeality, are always subject. During his earthly life Jesus was always somewhere to be found and seen for disciple and opponent, for friend and foe: "one" could say: "Look, there he is." Now this appears to be nowhere the case, neither by the witnesses who are enumerated in 1 Corinthians 15, 5–11 (even the "more than five hundred" of verse 6 are "brothers" and the Lord appeared when they were together), nor in the narratives of the apparitions of the gospels. An objectifiable ascertainment is, moreover, excluded by the words of Peter: "But God raised him . . . and made him manifest; not to all the peoples but to us who were chosen by God as witnesses" (Acts 10, 40b.).

Only in the faith does the heavenly Lord allow himself to be encountered, whether this encounter be described as seeing, feeling, or eating together. It will already be clear (and we shall be returning to this point immediately) that this by no means signifies subjectivism. It is certainly said that the resurrected Lord was known only in intersubjectivity, that seeing and feeling him did not convince by ascertainment, but brought to faith: for all the disciples, and most of all for Thomas and Saul. This is in itself no loss of reality in such contact, it is a gain. The Christ awakened by God does not stand to be looked at, but gives himself to be known; he appears only in the most profoundly personal way in communion with us and can be encountered only through personal acceptance, in the opening of the person to the faith. If we too were in the completed life, then this would mean nothing but riches. But the word "faith" already says that we stand on earth and are still in darkness. The risk of faith, which was described in the foregoing, also holds with regard to the risen Christ, indeed it holds precisely for him. Jesus has preceded us all on the path of faith and he has reached perfection on it, as the epistle to the Hebrews testifies. But we do not see him face to face in this perfection, our faith is also and precisely with regard to him the assurance of things hoped for, the conviction of things not seen (Hebrews 11, 1).

NOT PERSONALLY RESURRECTED?

In the foregoing we have eliminated some objections against belief in Jesus' resurrection and our own, that is, the idea of a return to and an endless continuation of our earthly form of existence. On the other hand, with the recognition of the radical nature of dying, something has also been taken from faith in a personal existence of the resurrected Lord that formerly seemed to be a support (in reality, however, a false support). For us today there is a new interest in this earthly life: after the Church now the world is awakened in our hearts, and this interest too can be a form of faith. It is then not surprising that present-day theology speaks more hesitantly of eternal life and also of the resurrected life of Christ. It does this particularly in the wake of the demythologizing and de-historizing exegesis of Rudolf Bultmann. The revived interest in Jesus' earthly life since Bultmann has not undone the scepticism concerning his resurrection and resurrected existence—quite the contrary. The study by Willi Marxsen on the resurrection as an historical and theological problem[58] can be considered a valid example of such questioning.

Marxsen rightly affirms that the resurrection itself was not witnessed by anyone (neither is it described anywhere in the canonical writings of the New Testament) and that the resurrected Lord himself is not to be approached historically. The only fact that stands inside our history and at the same time is accessible for historical investigation is what happened to the witnesses. All of those who, for example, are enumerated in 1 Corinthians 15, 5–8 had an experience which happened to them with regard to Jesus

58. W. Marxsen, *Die Auferstehung Jesu als historisches und als theologisches Problem*, Gütersloh, 1967. The same author exposed his idea more extensively in his book *The Resurrection of Jesus of Nazareth*, London, 1970. In the latter book it is clearer that the person of Jesus, and not only his "cause," is affirmed as present by Christian faith in the resurrection.

of Nazareth, who had died on the cross. What happened to them? He was seen by them or he showed himself to them (ὤφθη). When the witnesses proclaimed this fact, they interpreted it, they made use, in Marxsen's terminology, of a pattern of interpretation ("interpretament"). Marxsen thinks that we can even distinguish two such patterns. On the one hand, we can interpret the experience of the disciples by concluding to an event: he is arisen, God has awakened him. This interpretation or conclusion arises because a general conviction in Judaism, especially in Phariseeism, is here adapted to Jesus —that the dead will arise. According to Marxsen, Jesus' resurrection in 1 Corinthians 15 is a special case of the general resurrection. If, says Marxsen, the disciples had been Platonic Greeks, then they would probably have spoken only of the continued life of Jesus' soul. Thus far the first pattern, which Marxsen calls "personal." There is a second one, which he calls "functional." It consists in the beginning of a function. Those who experienced Jesus know that they are witnesses and preachers. It is Paul in particular who expresses this point, especially when, as in 1 Corinthians 15, 5–8, he does not insert himself in the ranks of the other witnesses, but speaks of his own experience, as he does in Galatians 1, 15f. That God "revealed his Son" to Paul drives him to preaching (Galatians 1, 23), and he can say, "Am I not an apostle? Have I not seen Jesus our Lord?" (1 Corinthians 9, 1). The apparition story in Matthew 28, 16–20 also mentions a task, a mission, without speaking—at least expressly—of the event of the resurrection itself. Marxsen's interest in this second pattern is particularly great. He gives a formula which can be considered his own definition of the functional interpretation, that is, *die Sache Jesu geht weiter* ("the cause of Jesus goes on"). But here it should be pointed out that Marxsen demonstrates at length that the "cause of Jesus" cannot be separated from his person, that this would make it a religion or ideology. It is not we alone who continue Jesus' cause, he himself comes to us, even today. Here we have the two patterns which Marxsen points out. He feels that they are still valid today, even the first. Whoever today is captured by Jesus' proclamation, by his "cause," can say: he is arisen. Marxsen's study was called in a first version: *Auferstehung Jesu—Ereignis oder Interpretament?* ("The Resurrection of Jesus—Event or Interpretation?"). This dilemma could be more closely described as: "*historisches Ereignis oder unverbindliches Interpretament?*" ("historical event or free interpretament?"). We do not think we are doing him any injustice if we formulate his answer to this question thus: the resurrection of Jesus is not a historical fact, it is one of the possible and therefore free ways to interpret what comes over us if we are seized by him after Jesus' death.

Marxsen's interpretation was reproduced here as a specimen of what many people feel and think concerning our own and Jesus' resurrection. Insofar as people do think of it, many reasons can be cited to explain the resurrection as a free interpretation of the fact that Jesus' influence somehow pervades. One can first of all think of doing justice to the Old Testament and thus also of entering into dialogue with modern Judaism. The Torah acknowledges only God's blessing or punishment in this earthly life, which is why the Sadducees, who hold only to the Torah, already in Jesus' and Paul's time denied the resurrection (Mark 12, 18 and par.; Acts 23, 8). The prophets show God's promise by predicting a restoration of the nation that will be like a resurrection from the dead (Ezekiel 37, 1–14), although in this case a collective resurrection. That everyone will get his share only emerges in apocalyptic theology (Daniel 12, 2f.) and is a Maccabean conviction (2 Maccabees 7, 9. 14. 23. 29. 36).[59] The wisdom of the Proverbs is still completely in the "here and how": just as in the Deuteronomist books "life" and "death" are forms of this earthly existence itself, whereas the actual dying is generally accepted as normal.[60] For Ecclesiastes death is a threat, but the joys of this life are God's blessings. The individual death in Israel is never presented as the beginning of a complete nothing, but "*sheol*" is still the lack of everything which gives life content: power, enjoyment of the fruits of work, communion with one's fellow man and even with God. The *sheol* after this life could, just as the chaos before the creation, be called a practical nothing. Only occasionally does God's power appear to penetrate this or his trust appear for us to reach across death. Only the

59. On the characteristics of prophetism and apocalyptic see Jürgen Moltmann, *Theology of Hope,* New York and London, 1967, pp. 124–138.
60. On the idea of death in Wisdom literature see N. Lohfink, *Das Siegeslied am Schilfmeer,* Frankfurt, 1965, pp. 198–243: "Der Mensch vor dem Tod."

chronologically last book of the diaspora canon, the book of Wisdom, openly expresses among the Wisdom books the conviction of Daniel and 2 Maccabees both the Greek idea that the soul remains and the Jewish-apocalyptic notion that immortality is a gift only of the resurrection: "But the souls of the righteous are in the hand of God, and no torment will ever touch them. In the eyes of the foolish they seemed to have died, and their departure was thought to be an affliction, and their going from us to be their destruction; but they are at peace. For though in the sight of men they were punished, their hope is full of immortality" (3, 1–4).

This conviction became, apart from the Greek strain in the book of Wisdom, common property in Palestinian Judaism. Its bearers were the Pharisees in particular. It is then best to understand that Paul, here remaining a Pharisee, speaks in 1 Corinthians 15 on Jesus' and our resurrection. Certainly, Christ is arisen and thus also now living. But, one could ask, does not the oldest eucharistic theology, to be found in Paul himself (1 Corinthians 11, 24–26) testify to a "remembrance of the Lord's death," much more than to a presence of his person? For this and similar reasons one might wonder whether there is not, within the faith in Jesus Christ, just as much room for a "Sadducaic" as for a "Pharisaic" interpretation of his influence. One could ask here: Is not the person of Jesus Christ the *one* new element of the New Testament, so that all attitudes which could find a place within the Old Testament faith in God are also legitimate within the faith in Christ? If this were true, then a purely "here and now" Christianity is also legitimate, and this has indeed long existed within Protestant liberalism and is now also beginning to express itself more and more openly among Catholics. In such "here and now" Christianity, hope in the eternal life would not alienate us from building a future on earth, while precisely the remembrance of Jesus' example constantly revitalized in preaching can give us the strength for our task.

PERSONALLY RISEN AND PERSONALLY PRESENT

We have intentionally, proceeding from Marxsen's exegesis, given a full description of an interpretation of Jesus' resurrection which stands diametrically opposed to the one that we first challenged—

the interpretation which sees this resurrection as nothing but a fact, as a historical and objectifiable fact. These two interpretations agree, or at least can agree, that God has given us in Jesus Christ his highest self-revelation and his ultimate salvation, and that God thus bestows in Christ ultimate future and hope, although it also becomes obvious how much both diverge in the idea of this future and of Christ's influence. Supporters of both ideas would first have to recognize one another's hope and have to find one another in the realization of this hope and in the construction of a world in peace and love. Then, however, the more profound differences can be discussed. Such a discussion we present here.

We have already pointed out that the resurrection of Jesus or, to put it more generally, his entry into glorified life, is *not* a historical and objectifiable fact. If Marxsen understands the interpretation "he is arisen" thus, he is right to reject it. Such an interpretation seems to us not free, but false. But this does not exclude the fact that "Easter" is an event, not only in the disciples but also in Jesus. This event can be real without being reducible to the product or the immanent content of our faith. The resurrected Lord can be present as person both for the first witnesses and for us, without being merely evoked by our memory. On the contrary, he can be primarily the one who calls us and brings us to belief. This is not only possible; we must and indeed may confess that it *is* so, that Jesus Christ thus lives in his completion and in us. This is testified by the first preaching and the whole New Testament, it is repeated by tradition, it is even now still the gospel on which we stand (1 Corinthians 15, 1).

The views of the newer exegesis and theology need not deny this point. On the contrary, they stand open for this message. Where Marxsen is concerned, it is remarkable how much he is fascinated by the difference between the two interpretations, and how little interest he shows for their concurrence. In most of the apparition narratives in the gospels, however, both the resurrection is testified to and a mission expressed. This is so in the final edition of Matthew 28, Luke 24, and John 20, although these chapters are compiled from various traditions. This is also the case with the compilative and synthesizing "longer Mark conclusion" (16, 9–20). Moreover, one can say that both of Marxsen's interpretations, merge in a third which is reproduced in Jesus' titles, especially in that of "Lord." That precisely the Crucified One is made Lord means that he rules and sends, but also that he exists as person in an ultimate way with God ("he sits on the right hand of the Father"), but thus calls the "chosen witnesses" to faith, which they can answer with the cry, "My Lord and my God" (John 20, 28). The sending Lord is person, for our faith but not merely through this faith.

This means that the personal "arisen-ness" of the Lord is not a free interpretation, but essentially belongs with God's salvation in Jesus Christ. The pluriformity of attitudes and views within the Old Testament cannot free us from the obligation of taking this New Testament salvific fact seriously. Indeed, is this pluriformity so free and indifferent within the Old Testament itself? First, it must be pointed out that the fantastic ideas which Jewish apocalyptic writings give of the other life, or the Hellenistic influence in the description of it which the book of Wisdom gives, need detract nothing from the authenticity of faith in, and hope for, eternal life itself. These are precisely inspired by faith in the God of salvation. We can say that this belief in God is the only one which distinguishes Israel and Judaism in a religious way from their cultural milieu, but it must be said here that this faith makes everything that is taken over gradually different and new: worship, one's outlook on nature and history, and finally also on death and the hereafter. God's salvation is so great that it reaches beyond death and man discovers finally that he may also personally trust in it. The God of Abraham, Isaac, and Jacob, the God of the Burning Bush, is not a God of the dead, but of the living. The passage in which this argument (*ad hominem*, because it is from the Torah itself!) is wielded against the Sadducees (Mark 12, 18–27 and par.) may possibly include the *ipsissima vox* of Jesus during his earthly life, and certainly it gives the correct Christian, and also the correct Jewish, evaluation of the development carried out in the Old Testament. The Catholic Church can then be thankful that in its acceptance of the Old Testament it does not base itself on the Palestinian canon alone.

However, the question of the Old Testament canon need not lead to schism for we find faith in the eternal life expressed unambiguously in the New Testament writings: in the just-mentioned passage and in everything that is said on Christ's resurrection and on his

161

return. Where 1 Corinthians 15 is concerned, Marxsen is correct when he says that Paul sees Jesus' resurrection as a special case of the general resurrection (see especially verses 13 and 16). But Marxsen overlooks precisely the special nature of Jesus' "case." It is for him not a matter of a resurrection on the day of judgment, but of an anticipation of it which has already occurred now, so that Jesus is the "first-fruits" (verses 20–24). The Jewish expectation of the resurrection does indeed then interpret the event with Jesus, but especially does the reverse takes place. Christ is "raised on the third day in accordance with the scriptures" (1 Corinthians 15, 4), but on the other hand the encounter with him as the Risen One gives us a new and deeper interpretation of the scriptures, which comes to the fore in Luke particularly (24, 27. 45). It can also be said of the New Testament that the person of Christ is the only new element, but again it must be added that he makes all the others new and different. This also holds for the remembrance of him. Where memory is led to Jesus, one proclaims his death, but by so doing one does not exclude his resurrection. In any case, the special nature of the eucharistic proclamation of the death of the Lord is that it happens "until he comes" (1 Corinthians 11, 26). That he will come means that he lives, although this is provisionally understood as being done in heaven (Acts 3, 21). As in the Old Testament, God was too great to be a God of the dead, so God's salvific presence in Jesus makes him alive for evermore (Revelation 1, 18).

The testimony of scripture gives us, therefore, more hope than God's salvation within this earthly life alone, for it testifies to Jesus not only as remembrance but as living person. This is not to say, however, that the Old Testament or modern culture have been simply overtaken in their "here and now" expectation of salvation. The old strands of the Old Testament continue to have meaning and can—even must—be integrated anew, as we have done in the foregoing reflections even with the older strands of the New Testament. Norbert Lohfink is largely in the right when he shows that expectation built on Jesus' resurrection of an eternal salvation already within the New Testament detracts from an attention to salvation on earth. Certainly, Jesus' preaching of the decision of faith and love continues to reach us today, but the space in which these can be elaborated was to a great extent obscured by the *Naherwartung* and the persecution situation. But even when, a long time afterwards, the persecutions ceased, the Church itself, more than the establishment of God's kingdom in the whole world, was the point on which the attention of the Church is focused. Certainly, it has done much for the cultural edification of Western Europe, but it was so intertwined with medieval society that an emancipation from the latter at the same time alienated Church and world from one another. A *diakonia* with a view to the salvation of the world without making it part of the Church only slowly came into view, first in the Reformation, and now in the Catholic Church as well, especially since Vatican II. It has brought room for an evaluation of a faith of worldly values and an exercise of love and thus a bringing of the kingdom of God into the profane area of history. We should never forget here the promise of an eternal life, but perhaps we can come to a full assent to this promise of an ultimate future only after we have said the penultimate word, which is concerned with salvation and future on earth. Then our faith in the glorified person of Jesus Christ will perhaps again take on a fuller meaning for us: we shall see him then more clearly as the source of all salvation and all love in this earthly time and as the one who draws us to the ultimate perfection which he himself has already reached, the foundation, perfection, and perfecter of our faith (Hebrews 12, 2), the first and the last (Revelations 1, 17).

Jesus is not *"auferstanden wie Goethe"* ("arisen as Goethe resurrected"), as someone has said in opposition to Bultmann,[61] who, moreover, does not seem to have reduced Jesus' "resurrection" to such a "rising." Jesus' glorified life and also our eternal life are not merely a "living on" in works and memory, they mean much more a personal life that is independent of both. But this personal continued existence does not render the continued existence in history worthless, and indeed it can perhaps be better understood from the basis of such historical living on. Living on in history is also something which is specifically human. The whole of material humanity already lives on to a certain degree in a retention of mass or energy. Living beings live on in their progeny, and germ cells are thus in a certain sense immortal. Moreover, all beings continue to

61. Gerhard Bergmann in *Der Spiegel* of April 11, 1966, p. 93.

emanate effects that have repercussions in space as well as in time. This is all present in man in a humanized manner. The Old Testament shows all sorts of ways in which man takes care to see that his good name continues to exist in his successors (even when relativized in Wisdom 3 and 4), and this is still true. Today men have more feeling for their qualitative development than for their quantitative expansion, so living on in works and history is a primary goal, and we Christians may not disparage this on behalf of the eternal life. Neither has the eternal life anything to gain by disqualifying this so human form of living on; on the contrary, the life of the dead and primarily the glorified life of Jesus Christ takes on a new significance if it is viewed from this living on in history. Then it appears greater. The continuation of someone's influence is just as unlimited in time and space as the influence of any kind of material life or happening, but at a given moment it becomes anonymous. The death of a beloved person initially causes his memory to be more intensified and purified, but this memory dies also in time. Even the great cultural creations eventually become anonymous: the individuality of their creators comes to be hidden behind an empty name—as with Homer or Shakespeare—or even the name has been lost. By contrast, both the fact and our faith guarantee that the name of Jesus is not lost. Tongues will confess him not merely in the "stages" of the universe, but also in the phases of history. Even God-is-dead theology appeared to have found him unforgettable.

Moreover, memory itself directs us to the personal presence which we may profess of Jesus for memory is evoked by the one who is remembering, but is based on a cognizance in which the known himself is also active. Memory of a person, at least as person, in personal contact, is based on the self-revelation through which a person gave himself freely to be known and entered in communion with us. When we remember a beloved person, we evoke in our innermost selves what he has given us of himself. Indeed, we surrender to the presence of this person in us, across time and space. For that reason, memory not only points back to the presence which once was, but it is also preserved by presence. And this not only upon seeing the person once again, which for the moment makes memory superfluous, but also through his unseen presence, when the beloved *continues* to bestow himself. Those who are seized by the memory of Jesus, who wish to celebrate his memory, can thus be open to the message that as person he lives and is present to evoke this remembrance.

Thus Marxsen—in interpreting the fact that "the cause of Jesus lives on"—cannot avoid mentioning the person of Jesus. He finds in Bultmann's words that "Jesus has risen into the kerygma" that the word "risen" (*auferstanden*) is misplaced; but he is prepared to accept Bultmann's further definition: "that Jesus is really present in the kerygma, that it is *his* Word which encounters the listener in the kerygma."[62] But does this mean that Marxsen—perhaps just as Bultmann himself—really *does* refuse to accept the resurrection as a historical, an inner-historical fact—as we too have refused to do—but that both are susceptible to a personal presence of the glorified Jesus in his community? In any case, Marxsen says, "It is then not a matter of arising into the kerygma, but of the presence of Jesus in the kerygma of his witnesses, of the *living* presence of the crucified Jesus."[63] Indeed, it is possible to conceive of this living presence as that of Jesus' "cause." But Marxsen immediately adds, "And the living on of the Jesus kerygma occurs in such a way that the old 'cause' introduced by Jesus is now no longer abstracted from him. The witnesses do not form any idea of it, no truths, which could be detached from Jesus, no ideology and no religion; but the living on of the Jesus kerygma always remains a living on of the *Jesus* kerygma."[64] Further on, Marxsen even attempts the formulation: "*He still comes today.*"[65] Or even: "He is the Risen One, because he (identically with the Earthly One) still today *comes* with the same (old) claim. But if I say this, then I must be clear in my mind that I do not necessarily have to employ the term 'the Risen One,' but do have to speak of the 'Living One.' And that actually means more . . ."[66] Further on still, Marxsen shows that it is not the arising in the historical sense that is the foundation of preaching, faith, and Church, but "the experience of seeing. But that produced a movement which I have always (formally) referred

62. Marxsen, *Die Auferstehung Jesu als historisches und als theologisches Problem* (note 58).
63. Marxsen, *op. cit.,* p .25.
64. Marxsen, p. 26.
65. Marxsen, p. 26.
66. Marxsen, p. 27.

to as the living on of 'Jesus' cause'—but which may not by any means be so thoughtlessly understood, as though it meant: We will just go on."[67] This latter pronouncement appears to be saying decisively that the presence, the life of Jesus itself, is active and cannot merely be reduced to our thoughts, memory, and so forth. It is possible that Marxsen, and especially an entire latent "memory christology," is here being interpreted too much according to the personal reality and presence of the glorified Christ.[68] But in any case, we feel that modern thought has strayed far less from the faith that Jesus lives than was at first supposed.

GLORIFIED PERSON AND GLORIFIED BODY

Jesus, who has ascended to his glory, thus lives personally. However, we must ask what precisely do we mean when we speak of his glorified person, and still more when we discuss his glorified body. In the first place, it is useful to establish what the introduction of the terms "person" and "body" is meant to reject. In "person" this aspect is clear: we name the glorified Christ a "person" in order to say that he cannot be reduced to the content or projection of our memory, is not called into existence by our faith but on the contrary evokes our faith, that he himself lives and makes himself present to us. Personhood in the Semitic idea of man self-evidently included corporeality. Only in the Hellenistic world

67. Marxsen, p. 34.

68. Reflecting on what I wrote here some years ago it seems to me that concerning the presence of Christ's person (and not only of his program or doctrine) in his community I share the idea of Willi Marxsen (see also note 58) and of other modern theologians. An opposition to some of them comes to the fore with regard to *our* resurrection. Does Christ's personal presence depend on the survival of his church or at least of the human race, or is Christ himself the principle of the resurrection unto a personal life after death? Modern thinking is prone to opt only for the first, as appears especially in a process theology like Peter Hamilton's *The Living God and the Modern World,* Philadelphia, 1967, pp. 211–234: "The Livingness of Jesus Christ." With all respect for the faithful approach of this author I cannot see that the merely objectifying "prehension" of Jesus into the mind (or "subsequent nature") of God (see also pp. 124–133) and the negation of a living on of Christ and of us as subjects is a satisfying interpretation of the Christian message. I know all the difficulties of speaking about this absolute and ultimate future, but an *exclusion* of such a future for human subjects seems to me to detract from "the scriptures and the power of God" (Mark 12, 24).

did this word become a problem: hence in 1 Corinthians 15, Paul speaks on the one hand of the resurrection of the body, but on the other hand sharply distinguishes between the resurrected body and the earthly body. Since then, up to and including the conflict with the Albigenses in the Middle Ages, bodily resurrection has always been in the fore, even in terms which do not seem to take much into account the oppositions of 1 Corinthians 15, 42–44, as when the fourth Lateran Council says that the dead will arise with the same bodies that they now have (DS 801: *"cum propriis resurgent corporibus, quae nunc gestant"*). But theology has never denied the distinction between the earthly and glorified body; on the contrary, it has always, in some way or other, elaborated it, so that we have primarily to conceive of the identity of the earthly and arisen body as a concretization of the identity between earthly and arisen person. Nothing of what is *proper* to us disappears. Corporeality and association with the earth are not something *from* which, but on the contrary something *with* which and *in* which, we will be ultimately redeemed. Precisely to the degree in which they are *proper* to us (*"cum propriis resurgent corporibus"*), to the degree in which they are integrated in our person, may we arise with corporeality and earthly association, as Christ arose with them.

Certainly, this latter point contains an entire speculation on the glorified person and corporeality. Before we go further, however, yet another observation must be made on the whole character of our knowledge concerning the eternal life. Our concepts on this life are, just as with those on God, positive and yet at the same time negative. We express perfection of God, but without creatural limitation, so that finally we clumsily express ourselves concerning God in words with prefixes like all- and un-: all-knowing and unlimited. Equally, when we speak of eternal life, earthly life is our point of departure: eternal life is, then, fullness of the earthly life, but without the limitations of, for example, mortality and corruptibility, unpersonal objectifiability, disintegration in time. For that reason, eternal life cannot simply be called the "here*after*," for such an expression places it and the other life within the same time sequence. Moreover, all such expression, just as with those on God, are not merely or primarily *about* God, but are a speaking *to* him. To speak about God is to confess him, and to speak of the final completion is a confession of our absolute hope in God. This is

167

true of our confession of Jesus' resurrection and glorification. But then we are also and at the same time expressing the foundation of this hope as a reality now present for us. For that reason, then, we shall further briefly discuss the person and body of the Resurrected One.

When earlier we discussed the question of Christ's human or divine person, we considered personhood first of all as an existing-in-itself, and indeed in such a way that this has developed to conscious self-possession and free cause. Personhood here implies something that is individual, what the customary scholastic definitions wished to express by using the word *"incommunicabilis."* However, it is better to use the word "inalienable" than "incommunicable," for in love precisely the person communicates himself, and furthermore only loving self-communication to the other makes the man fully a person. For that reason, the person ultimately perfected in the eternal life must also be regarded as a person who communicates himself in and from God precisely to others. Now we may confess the glorified Christ as the first perfected person. This means that his life with God (Romans 6, 10) is just as much a life with us to the close of the age (Matthew 28, 20), and in this close itself (Revelations 21, 22; 22, 3). Or, as we already said above, Christ's heaven is his salvific power on earth. He is not a redeemer in retirement, but he completes his redemption, just as his Father does, by being active precisely in his sabbath rest (Genesis 2, 2–3; John 5, 17). His gift *"for the many"* in the sacrifice on the cross (Mark 10, 45 and par.; 14, 24 and par.) has become in his glorification a self-giving *to* the many. That the Spirit is gift and distributor of gifts does not detract at all from this fact, for "the Lord is the Spirit" (2 Corinthians 3, 17). The Spirit makes him present as giving and working, the Spirit is the "representative" of the glorified Christ, which is not to say that he comes in place of him, but precisely that he makes Christ himself present in any place where the Spirit is poured out.

Thus the person of the Glorified One also defines his corporeality. Body is not here to be understood as the accumulative cells or molecules which the man had during his earthly life—this too, for that matter, is not a stable entity, though it is "individual" only to ourselves. We shall arise with our "own" body insofar as it has become our "own" during our own history. We shall be raised up

168

not with that body which needs food at one time and excretes it at another, but with that body which is made pure or impure, holy or unholy, by our heart, that is, by the depths of our person (Matthew 15, 17f.). Thus it is primarily with Christ himself. Whatever one might think of the historicity of the empty grave, the body of the Lord in which he encounters his disciples is important. According to Luke (24, 39f.) and more clearly still in John (20, 20. 27), the Risen One showed his wounds, the signs of the suffering on the cross that completed his life sacrifice, and he appeared to his disciples thus as the Lamb that is slaughtered (Revelations 5, 6). Thus the risen body of the Lord is the expression of the person which he was and became in his earthly life. We may call this risen body his own to the degree that thereby he is not objectifiable for others but is completely free subject: he does not stand on view, but gives himself to be known.

Body, as that piece of world which is individual to the person, has no clear limit even in our earthly existence. If not biologically, then certainly anthropologically, one makes "the other" an extension of one's body, an embodiment of oneself: as in clothing and home. But one also makes a beloved person one's own body, not however by adapting it or securing it, but by transmitting oneself to it. We can speculate on a completion of this process in the eternal life. It is not unthinkable, on the contrary it is even probable, that the person completed in the eternal life lives in our world, in us. Thus it would appear that precisely the glorified Jesus lives on earth. Seen thus, the glorified body of Christ is extended to those in whose hearts he dwells through faith (Ephesians 3, 17). Then the Church is in an extremely real sense Christ's body—not only in a figurative, but also in the literal sense. Here it should be noted that the term "*mystical* body of Christ" was transferred to the Church not by Paul, nor even by the patristic tradition, but only in the Middle Ages, and indeed on the basis of the Eucharist, which for us today is primarily the gift of Christ's "real" body.[69] In this concept, Christ's "own" or "individual" body—insofar as there can in the glorification still be question of it—would extend to his Church, indeed both would coincide.

This is not to say that *Christ* coincides with his Church.

69. H. de Lubac, *Corpus mysticum: L'Eucharistie et l'Eglise au moyen âge,* Paris, 1944.

Already in our earthly life our person is opposed to the body in spite of all attempts at identification: We freely manipulate the reality which on the other hand we ourselves are. For the completion we can imagine that the freedom through which we transcend the reality which is our body is complete, together with our immanence in and our identification with this reality. For Christ this would mean that he stands sovereign and free with regard to his Church, and on the other hand is more inwardly bound to her and identified than I am now with my own body. Primarily it was Paul who brought this sovereignty to expression in the captivity epistles, where Christ is Lord and Head of his Church, whereby "Head" is not primarily to be understood as a biological image, but as ruler, chief, as Christ is also Head of all rule and authority (Colossians 2, 10) and the husband is the head of the wife (Ephesians 5, 23). The image of Christ as Head and the Church as his body is paralleled in Ephesians, 5, 22–33 by that of bridegroom and bride, or rather of husband and wife, and indeed it could even be that this image lies at the foundation of that of head and body,[70] through which the duality in oneness, and thus the transcendence of Christ, still more clearly emerges. This concept of Christ's glorified body, which identifies that body with the Church, has the advantage of underlining still further the unity between Christ's existence with the Father and among us, and thus the unity between personal continued existence and life in history; while on the other hand it does not cause the person of the glorified Christ to be absorbed in us. Until now we have ignored the eucharistic texts on Christ's body. However, it should be said concerning them that we, in the Eucharist with Christ himself, also receive one another, so that it becomes still clearer that we who receive this one Bread all together form one body (1 Corinthians 10, 17), and that "discerning the body" (*ibid.*, 11, 29) must at the same time be understood as of the eucharistic and the Church-body of Christ.[71]

70. P. Andriessen, "La nouvelle Eve, corps du nouvel Adam," in *Aux origines de l'Eglise,* Paris, 1965, pp. 87–109.

71. See Augustine, *Sermo* 272: *"Corpus ergo Christi si vis intelligere, apostolum audi dicentem fidelibus: 'Vos autem estis corpus Christi et membra'* (1 *Cor.* 12, 27). *Si ergo vos estis corpus Christi et membra, mysterium vestrum in mensa dominica positum est: mysterium vestrum accipitis."*

THE FUTURE OF CHRIST

We shall complete this reflection on Christ's glorified existence with a note on its beginning and continuance. We have already said that this life is never—not even in the apparitions—a repetition of Jesus' earthly life. The difference between the way in which the disciples knew him before and after the ascension seem completely "from their side": either in the structure of their experience, or in its literary reproduction. The ascension is thus the last apparition, and this too only for the Twelve and their entourage, whereby the ascent is either experience or literary expression. But it is striking that only Acts 1, 3 states a period of forty days between resurrection and ascension; other texts place the ascent of Christ immediately after the apparition on the day of resurrection (Luke 24, 51; Mark 16, 19), and John even speaks of it before the first apparition to the Eleven (20, 19); while, apart from the texts cited here, scarcely a distinction is elsewhere made between the resurrection and the ascension (Acts 2, 32f.; Ephesians 1, 20, and the whole of Hebrews). What holds for the relation between resurrection and ascension can be extended to the sending of the Spirit and even to Jesus' death on the cross. The sending of the Spirit is placed in Acts 2, 1 at Pentecost, thus on the fiftieth day after the Jewish passover feast; in Acts 2, 33, however, the distance in time is lacking, and in John the Spirit is communicated by the just risen Lord (20, 22), even by the dying Christ in the breath which he "gave up" (19, 30), as also by the water from his pierced side (19, 34; see 7, 38f.).

This latter also indicates a coincidence of Jesus' entry into his glorification with the death itself. It is true that from the time of the oldest kerygma (1 Corinthians 15, 4) Jesus' resurrection "on the third day" was spoken of (Acts 10, 40; in the gospels insofar as the "first day of the week" is inclusively reckoned the third day after Jesus' death). Here too it holds that the distance in time existed on the side of the disciples: again either in their experience or in literary representation. The latter is probable because of the connection of "on the third day" and "according to the scriptures" in the old kerygmatic formulation of 1 Corinthians 15, 4 in various confessions of faith. "The scriptures" speak of God's salvation on the third day or after three days in 2 Kings 20, 5, Jonah 1, 17 (see Matthew 12, 40), and Hosea 6, 2; and in the latter text even of an arousing from the dead. After all, Jesus' resurrection itself, or his entry into glorified existence, is for that matter described nowhere in the New Testament. To see it as the positive side of one event that has its negative side in the death on the cross is to reach an accord not merely with what has just been said on the Spirit on Jesus' death on the cross, but also with two other concepts from St. John's gospel: that Jesus' "elevation" or "exaltation" is at the same time his crucifixion and his glorification (3, 14; 8, 28; 12, 32; see 18, 32), and that both are included in the one going to the Father (16, 28).

Whether or not Jesus remained for three days in the grave is, apart from what one thinks of the empty grave, no obstacle to such an idea of unity. The grave never contained Jesus, nor Jesus' body, but his corpse. When one says that the Word also dwelt in Jesus' body, or even that this body was assumed by the person of the Word, then this does not hold for Jesus' "body" in the grave. For as the Lord died a genuine death, his body did not remain on earth, only the *corpse,* essentially distinguished from that body by a "substantial change" (*mutatio substantialis*), that is, through the loss of its "form" (*forma substantialis*). Therefore, the predicates on the body are no longer applicable to the corpse. Neither need "descent into hell" present any difficulty against the unity of death and resurrection. As we have already said, it is primarily a strong expression for Jesus' actual death. That Jesus' death, his "completion," has meaning for the righteous ones before him—a thought which is more clearly expressed in Hebrews 11, 39—12, 2 than in Peter 3, 19f.—need not necessarily be ascribed to the departed soul of Christ, but can also emanate from the Christ glorified in his bodily reality.

If the Glorified One has meaning and salvific influence in the other life, then he also has such on earth. Let us extend this statement with a few remarks. The first concerns the role of our faith. We have until now emphasized the fact that it is not our belief which causes Jesus to rise up, but that the Risen One presents himself to our faith. It is not we who evoke him, but he who calls us to faith. This calling, however—and this must now be stated emphatically—demands an answer. The communion which the Risen One offers us comes about only through the answer of our faith. Christ lives in our hearts, in the heart of his Church, and thereby in the world, and this through the faith, hope, and love of all of us. This does not mean that the resurrected Christ is first of all living and that only in the second instance do we propagate his influence. Such is the case with no one, let alone with a person in his final completion. We have for that reason described the person of Christ as self-giving and his body as the Church. As the expression "the body of Christ" is not a mere image for a corporation which can be compared in a metaphorical sense with the "physical" body of the Lord, so too is it Jesus' own body and own person which grows in his Church and through his Church in the world. "I am Jesus, whom you are persecuting," says the Lord to the Saul who is killing his disciples (Acts 9, 5). Can he also say to us, "I am Jesus, who causes you to speak and act"?

Thus the risen Christ still has hope and still future. The first expression can sometimes be found among Catholic theologians, the second emerges from the reflections of Moltmann.[72] On one point they agree: Christ has, even in his completion, still hope for the future which is his completion in us. For that reason, such Catholic authors ascribe to the glorified Jesus, as also to the dead, the divine virtue of hope before the parousia. We agree with this point insofar as one speaks not only of a glorified hope, but also of a glorified faith, that is, insofar as surrender to and the leaning upon God is meant thereby, while the earthly unfulfillment has fallen away. In glorified hope this unfulfillment has fallen away only for the individual person: the blessed now, the "souls under the altar" from Revelations, must wait "until the number of their fellow servants and their brethren should be complete" (6, 11), and thus the glorified Christ also awaits his brothers and limbs. The only thing that makes this theological opinion a somewhat solitary idea within Catholic thought is the fact that it ascribes a social

72. For the Catholics see, for example, P. Charles, "Spes Christi," in *Nouv. Revue théol.* 61 (1934), 1009–1021; 64 (1937), 1057–1075; J. Moltmann, *Theology of Hope*, pp. 139–229: Chapter 3: "The Resurrection and the Future of Jesus Christ."

character to hope, while in general Catholic theology ascribes the individual salvation of the hoping one only to the object of the virtue of hope. This difference, however, is more terminological than real, for it is generally assumed that by virtue of Christian love one may and must pray for the salvation of others. Such praying, however, includes the longing for and the expectation of salvation from God, and these are the two components of hope. For that reason there is nothing against, and everything in favor of, understanding the prayer of the blessed for us as their hope for our salvation. Especially is the glorified Christ always hoping for the salvation of all because "he always lives to make intercession for them" (Hebrews 7, 25).

What further does Christ hope for us? The authors whom we have so far discussed, would answer first of all: our completion, our blessedness, whereby they naturally include the grace necessary for this completion in this earthly life. Theologians such as Moltmann would first of all establish a relation to God's kingdom on earth. God's kingdom grows through Christ's witnesses, which is salvation for all, and precisely therein lies Christ's future and hope. This must first of all be fully affirmed by us. Jesus not only prophesied God's kingdom for the future but proclaimed and offered it in the present. Only from his earthly history and in this history has Christ been glorified in the eternal life, and this will also be true for us. We have confessed Jesus' glory in the struggle for belief in resurrection and eternal life in general. The most profound reason why modern man has difficulty with this recognition of faith lies in the fact that Christian preaching has for such a long time practically omitted the penultimate phase of salvation, namely, the earthly. Only a Christ who has a future in this life will also be the Center in the final completion of the kingdom of God. We know that the final completion of the individual person passes beyond death, but of the final completion of humanity and world we cannot form an image. The apocalyptic images show us a future aeon, which is in almost every aspect the opposite of the present one; but the New Testament also sees in Christ now, already, the end of the present evil age (Galatians 1, 4) and the presence of the eternal life (John 3, 26). For that reason, the breakthrough occurs of the final completion in Christ's parousia not merely from outside, but also from within.[73] Thus finally the glorified Christ, in and to whom everything is created (Colossians 1, 16), stands for us as the Endpoint to which everything moves but which also grows in everything, "the First and the Last, who died and came to life" (Revelations 2, 8).

73. See P. Teilhard de Chardin, *The Divine Milieu,* New York and London, 1964.

Conclusion

Is God Dead? —He Is a God of Men

THE patient reader will, I hope, have taken note of what was stated in the Introduction: both studies in this book are based on the same idea. God does not compete; the dilemma of "God or world?", "God or man?" is a false dilemma. Our concluding section can begin by making this still clearer in connection with the second, the christological study.

It is not superfluous to say that the question of "God or Jesus?" is also a false dilemma. In this book *A New Interpretation of Faith,* Thomas Sartory puts the question in a somewhat weakened form. There are believers, he says, for whom God is all and Jesus' position becomes a question, while others proceed from Jesus Christ and only thus come to God. The first choice is that of Jewish Christianity and for anyone who approaches the New Testament from the Old; it is also that of Sartory himself, who thinks that this approach will help the controversies between Reformation and Catholicism out of their difficulties. The second choice seems to be that of the mainstream of Christian tradition; it was accentuated in the christocentric theology of Karl Barth. In a much sharper way the dilemma of "God or Jesus?" comes to the fore in two modern Protestant theologians in the United States. S. M. Ogden states in his book *Christ Without Myth* that for us Christians it is not actually a matter of Jesus but of the God who is proclaimed by Jesus. By contrast, Paul van Buren in *The Secular Meaning of the Gospel* is completely agnostic towards any assertion concerning God himself and puts even Jesus' utterances on God down to his time-conditioned *Weltanschauung,* while on the other hand the person of Jesus and

176

his freedom is *the* inspiration of the Christian: here we find the christocentrism of Barth less the latter's theology.

Whoever finds the good news concerning Jesus Christ primarily in Matthew, Mark, Luke, and John—and not like Thomas Altizer in Blake, Hegel, and Nietzsche—must explain the question of "God or Jesus?" as a false dilemma. For the synoptics, Jesus is totally the bringer of God's kingdom and the one obedient to God's will; even the most striking self-pronouncements which John puts in Jesus' mouth always reveal him as living from the Father and to the Father. From the other side these Johannine self-pronouncements find their roots in the synoptics and in the appearance of Jesus himself, insofar as he shows awareness that in his own actions the kingdom of God is dawning. The Church has then always tried to confess, besides Christ's nearness of God, his full humanity, especially when it added in Chalcedon to the "of one substance with the Father" the "of one substance with us."

Chalcedon, however, also indicates the difficulty it cost the community of faith not to make God and Jesus one another's rivals. This difficulty can also be seen in scripture itself, as in St. John's gospel, where Jesus on the one hand possessed life in himself and yet had received it from the Father (5, 26). Or in the hymn of Philippians 2, where Jesus Christ receives the honor which in Isiah 45, 23 is reserved for God alone, while on the other hand he is confessed "to the glory of God the Father" (2, 11). The recognition of a divine person in Jesus makes him in himself not a rival of the Father, for this person is precisely the Son, who is indeed of one substance with the Father, but through being born from his substance, as Nicea says. Nevertheless, this reaction against Arianism in the East opened the way to a liturgical cult of Jesus which obscured his mediatorship. The second Arian conflict, which was mainly fought in the West Gothic Church of Spain, produced a doctrine of the Trinity in which the distinction between Father and Son was hidden even more completely behind their unity of substance—and their unity as principle of the Holy Spirit: the *"Filioque"*! In the piety of the Western Middle Ages Christ easily became then simply "God." The ambiguity of the title "Our dear Lord" still shows today the results of this piety. It is then understandable that both the liberal theology of the Reformation and all sorts of assertions of modern Catholics protest against the deification of Jesus.

But Jesus need not be understood as God's rival. The popular ideas of the West and the cult expressions of the East which concentrate on his divine person never deny that he is the *Son*. The eternal Son need nowhere "outshine" the Father, for he is completely from the Father. The doctrine of the Trinity of the West, and still more that of the East, which first look at the persons and only then at their one substance, explain the person of the Son as emanating in all his individuality from, directed towards, and transparent towards the Father. The reproach against this theology (at least if one prescinds from the way in which it is popularly handed down), that it makes Christ a rival of God, is not justified. The doctrine of the Trinity need not be contested on this point, and the christological study of this book is not directed against it.

But there remains one point on which the doctrine of Christ as God's eternal Son does evoke questions and justifies protests, and it is on this point that our christology is concentrated. The Christ who is God's eternal Son, of one substance with him, threatens to become dehumanized, the man in him risks being undermined to the benefit of the divine person. This occurred in Apollinarism and Monophysitism before Chalcedon; it also occurred in the christology after this council insofar as the one person of Christ as divine person makes his human reality anhypostatic, impersonal; indeed, it still happens today in the image of Christ with which many of us are brought up. We have accused this post-Chalcedonian image of Christ of being a secret denial of the "consubstantial with us" that Chalcedon itself pronounced. We have also avoided this denial without falling from the Scylla of Eutyches into the Charybdis of Nestorius. And we hope not to have detracted anything from the divinity of Jesus Christ through having raised questions concerning the pre-existent divine person.

Concerning the latter point, it was indeed tempting simply to adapt here the attitude of our first study by saying: divine person or human person is a false dilemma. But the dilemma was, precisely with regard to Christ's person, not to be resolved by putting "and" in place of "or": in this way we would have found ourselves again in the Nestorian Charybdis. For although the divine and the created are not numerable, they do have a relationship of dialogue.

On the one hand, all the human element comes to Jesus and he is therefore no less personal than we; on the contrary, he is more personal. If he is now, on the other hand, also a divine person, then no dialogue can be assumed between the divine and the human person within the one Christ such as between Christ and the Father. The divine person of the Word cannot be a "counterpart" of the man Jesus, as the Father is. The Word is then person—and is the Son—not over against the man Jesus but *in* him, the Word is enhypostatic in the man who is the Christ, the Son of the living God. Of God's inner Words outside Christ—or outside the history of salvation, which according to Hebrews 1, 1f. is a history of the utterances of God that come to completion in Christ—nothing can be said. In other words, even a *Logos asarkos* can in faith and theology only be conceived as *Verbum incarnandum*. God is three in one in his self-giving to us and he is eternally three in one insofar as this self-giving springs from his most original essence and his deepest heart.

He is a God of men. As God of men we know him in Israel and in Jesus Christ. This does not mean that a rational, "natural" answer of our affirmation of God is superfluous. On the contrary, this is necessary in order not to let our secularization turn into atheism. Proceeding from the secular, especially from the human reality, we are directed towards the supporting Foundation, the driving Will which always realizes it. But if we surrender to the human reality in its highest and most profound form, to the Fellow Man Jesus Christ, then only is our affirmation of God filled with inexpressible riches. With justifiable exaggeration, Pascal expresses this view when he opposes the God of the philosophers with the God of Abraham and of Christ or when he says that without Jesus Christ we can know neither God nor man. But Tillich's idea that the God of the philosophers is indeed the God of Abraham is also true, for the Foundation and Will which we already affirm from the world is shown in Israel and in Jesus as Love. The attributes which we acknowledge to God in a metaphysical reflection on our rational affirmation of God come in our faith completely under the criticism of the Love of God, through which he gives his Son for us, the Love of God in the countenance, even in the dying countenance of Jesus, the Love with which he wishes to be a God of men.

Let us offer one example. On the basis of any affirmation of God

we can call God "almighty." Our earthly reality is laden with power
and life, we humans experience our power with regard to nature
even in our own essence—how much more, then, must God be
recognized as powerful. For precisely as God he must be called
all-powerful or almighty. On the other hand, we cannot, just as little
as with other attributes, define the extent or content of this total
might, for we are not in the place of God himself. We can say that
God is mighty with regard to everything that is meaningful and
coherent in the world, but we cannot, for example, say that God, if
he is almighty, ought to have removed suffering, for it is possible
and probable that suffering is indissolubly connected with a becoming world. But in Jesus, God shows the direction of his power, which
was hidden from us. When we are told that Jesus has healed the
sick and awakened the dead, then it is revealed in him that God's
power does not direct us to suffering and death, but to life, in all
the fullness that this word contains in the Bible. But still more is
revealed in Jesus: God's total might wishes even to bear suffering
that emanates from the becoming world and from our sins, God is
mighty in order to pass through our death, his power shows to full
advantage in weakness and gives us life from death. The man Job
had to take back his reproaches against God because God's power
was a totally impenetrable secret. The Christian man finds, on the
one hand, the mystery of suffering and evil in the becoming world
itself, and on the other hand the mystery of God's might in the love
with which he is so much on our side that he takes our weakness,
even to our death, upon himself.

What holds for our philosophical divine attributes of God holds
also for the titles which were given to God in divine worship in the
Old and even in the New Testament. The word "almighty" in the
first article of many creeds is a perhaps not very apt translation of
παντοκράτωρ, Pantocrator, the All-ruler, he who has everything in
his power. This title refers to God as Lord, a title which in the New
Testament is also broadly attributed to Jesus. The religious and even
the philosophical man sees God in the prolongation of the king, the
governor. In Jesus we see not only the limitations of such a metaphor
more clearly, but also that it must be reversed. "To serve God is to
rule," says the adage, but God's own rule becomes service in Jesus.
When Israel matured in exile, it describes the ideal image of the

Servant of Yahweh. He is a prophet with no other power but that of his message, and in his death he becomes the salvation of the many. Jesus also appeared as a prophet, so that either he himself or the first Palestinian community understood him as this Servant. His non-violent appearance, his association with sinners and outcasts, his own rejection partly because of this association, the salvific meaning which he acknowledges to his death in the Last Supper, all this shows him as the fulfillment of the ideal image from Deutero-Isaiah. By all this Jesus is also the fulfillment of the messianic expectation, but the image of the Messiah King must be basically corrected if it is to be applied to him. Jesus himself rejected the earthly rule of a Messiah. What the community, probably above all that of Hellenistic Judaism, recognized in him is a heavenly rule, a sitting on the right hand of God, until God has laid low the enemies of his Christ at the latter's feet. Here too—precisely here in fact—is a reinterpretation applicable, and more or less clearly begins to be given in the New Testament. The subjection of the enemies means that he makes us free from the powers; where the Spirit of the Lord is, there is freedom. We could also express this point more radically: Jesus' Lordship is the sealing of his Servanthood. He has become historically powerful as Servant, he is the slaughtered Lamb who opens the scroll. Jesus' resurrection does not mean reanimation but glorification, but this glorification must be de-glorified in the recognition of the Spirit of service and self-giving which comes from him to us. But then God de-glorifies himself too in Jesus. He appears to be greater than our concepts of rule, he is just as much a serving God. Whoever thinks that this view ascribes a subordination to God should consider that rule also entails a counter-position. God's ruling is so much to our pure good, his glory lies so much in what he bestows on us, that he may be called a God of service, of self-emptying. He is the highest Ego, but not an Ego that concentrates everything in itself, but which says "thou" to all: "I want you to be yourselves and nothing more." He is a God of men.

God of men: we must also interpret the attributes which metaphysics ascribe to him and the titles which religious worship give to him. In this connection we shall also attempt to interpret the doctrine of God's three-in-oneness. Karl Rahner, in an inspiring reflection on

181

the doctrine of the Trinity (*The Trinity*, New York and London, 1970), has elaborated the trinitarian theology wholly in terms of the identity of immanent and economic Trinity. God's own, in him immanent (and thus precisely transcendent for us) threefoldness is his threefoldness in our history of salvation. Rahner adds to this: "and vice versa." Perhaps in our own christological study, such a "and vice versa" has been more sharply emphasized. This was at least done with regard to Father and Son. For that reason we shall now say a few words on the Holy Spirit.

Only in connection with the risen Christ, as gift of his glorification, is the Spirit shown us in the New Testament as "third person." But an individual third person of God's and Christ's Spirit is far from clear in the New Testament. The Word did not appear to be a person over against Jesus Christ but only in him over against the Father; with the Spirit, however, rather is the reverse the case. He is person over against Jesus' community and every man, but whether he also stands as person over against God and Christ remains in question. Certainly, in the Old Testament the spirit of Yahweh is his powerful working, and many places in the New Testament—especially where there is talk of πνεῦμα ἅγιον without article—give the same impression. As concerns the distinction of persons between Christ and the Spirit, John shows this very strongly in the farewell discourses, where Jesus proclaims the coming of the "other Paraclete," but for Paul the arisen Lord has become life-giving spirit, indeed "the Lord is the Spirit" (2 Corinthians 3, 17). Tradition also shows traces of this identification especially in so-called pneumachristology. For these reasons we may for the moment say that God, and precisely God himself, is in his salvific history not only Father and Son, but Father, Son, and Spirit. Again, on God's inner life apart from the salvific history brought about by him we have no knowledge, but on the other hand we can name God himself in his own depth and eternity no other than as he has given himself. As the Word was always expressing itself even to becoming flesh, so the spirit bestows itself to inhabiting. We may call the fullness of God's essence triune because he leads us as Father, Son, and Spirit to fullness.

"Is God dead? —He is a God of men." We have given this title to our concluding remarks because the image of God sketched here, especially of God's Trinity, can be an answer to the—or rather a—theology of "the death of God." Or perhaps what is sketched here says something of what some of the "God-is-dead" theologians have also wished to say, or for that matter others who proclaim a new image of God.

Of the latter we are thinking of Pierre Teilhard de Chardin, who was undoubtedly more prophet than theologian. He had nevertheless a deep theological vision which lies at the foundation of his whole world-view, that is, the orientation of the whole developing cosmos to the total Christ. For that reason Teilhard wished, as he himself several times expressed it, to replace the biblical God of above with the God of before, "*le Dieu d'en-avant*." But he did not see how much in the scriptures themselves, especially in the prophetic utterances, God is a God who is in front of us, a God of the future, and how especially the Spirit is God's power which steers to perfection. In positing "*le Dieu d'en-avant*" Teilhard opposed more specifically the God of behind, the God who stands only at the beginning, the God who *has* created. This has been more fully elaborated by theologians inspired by Teilhard than by Teilhard himself, especially by A. Hulsbosch in his book *God's Creation*.

Apart from Teilhard and the God who is in front of us is Thomas J. J. Altizer, who is against the God of the beginning. He is not the only "God-is-dead" theologian but he differs from the others in that he is certainly the most radical and the most visionary. His book *The Gospel of Christian Atheism* remains arresting even if one rejects it. Altizer can also be called the most radical prophet of religionless Christianity, for religion is for him completely related to the God of the beginning; this he borrows from Mircea Eliade. Altizer finds the most radical opposite pole of Christianity not in Platonic or Eastern dualism, but in the tendency inherent in all systems which find their source in India, the tendency to return, ascend, or descend with all the visible into the primordial ground of being. The biblical Creator and Judge are interpreted by Altizer as this absorbing primordial mystery. The redemptive message of Christianity is then that this God has died in Jesus, radically and irrevocably: from being transcendent he has become immanent, no longer a God who absorbs, alienates, or subjects us, but now a God who is Jesus, which ultimately means that God coincides with humanity "the Great Humanity Divine," as Altizer calls it, quoting

William Blake. The liberating element of this process is proclaimed partly in Nietzschean terms, and the process of God's dying itself is described on a Hegelian basis. The Absolute Spirit alienates itself from itself and thus comes to itself, and this self-alienation is the one kenotic event of God's becoming man and dying in Jesus and in humanity.

It is striking that Altizer does not mention the Lutheran authors of kenotic christology. They uphold the Logos, and more still the Father, as distinct divine persons, which Altizer would call not radical and not dialectic. It is even more striking that the kenosis hymn of Philippians 2, 6–11 does not appear among the very sparse scriptural quotations to be found in Altizer's work. The reason for this fact lies in Altizer's abhorrence of the resurrection and especially of the glorification and ascension of Christ. In this, however, the Church—whose distinct existence is in contradition with the Christian message—has turned back the whole event of God's self-emptying in accordance with religion by identifying the dead Jesus again with the primal mystery of God. While others do not take the death of Jesus seriously by ascribing to the Resurrected One a repetition of the earthly life, for Altizer, in the confession of the resurrection and glorification, the death of God is nullified in Jesus because God's original essence is ascribed again to the risen Lord. Christianity must be freed of this religion. It must live not on the hope in a God who is before, but on the good news that the God of the beginning has died in the divine humanity.

A refutation of Altizer demands internal, sympathetic criticism, and this would probably lead us to a consideration of Hegel. For that a new book is necessary. Yet if we have evoked the ideas of Altizer, then it is in order, first of all, to see whether our own ideas can also contribute to the discussion on what is called the death of God. We should like only to ask two questions which proceed respectively from the first and second part of this book.

The first question is whether Altizer's book is not written completely from the image of the competing God, even of the absorbing God. This God did indeed die in Jesus, he is constantly reawakened to life by us Christians, but he must die completely and will also die in the modern Western cultural situation, which will in this sense produce a religionless Christianity. Here, however, it is a matter of the annihilation on an *image* of God, making the death of God primarily a sociological phenomenon, as is the case for another American, Gabriel Vahanian. Already metaphysically we can see that God himself, if he precisely wishes to be God, does not compete. He showed this to be the case in an extreme way and shows it still in Christ. Only after this purification of our thought may we come to discuss the relations between God and his creation. Then one can affirm that everything is totally from the world and thus no less totally from God. Then the creation need not be limited to the beginning, and indeed it may not. Then the image of God who stands only at the beginning will be broken, but precisely to give way to a metaphysical but also a biblical concept of God's creation. The world and man will be fully there, they will be able to celebrate their liberation from any restriction by an image of God, from any idols, even the Christian ones, but it will be by God himself who radiated in the countenance of Jesus Christ. God himself involves himself in his creation and alters himself in these involvements: one can assume this without being Hegelian. He becomes triune—or more triune, or more expressly triune—towards and in his creation, but remaining God. He empties himself, but is precisely thus the God who makes life.

Thus we come to our second question, whether Altizer would not do well to include the Christian message of Jesus' glorification and the mission of the Spirit in his thought. We even wonder whether Altizer, in his study of Hegel, has given enough attention to the third phase of the absolute spirit, namely, that this comes to itself through alienation; but this question we are happy to relinquish to the experts. In any case, we think that the New Testament and also the Christian tradition offer to Altizer and to all of us many more reasons for celebrating the death of the God of religion with the real God. This God has indeed become man in Jesus and died our death. One may pronounce the controversial slogan, "One of the Trinity has suffered," one can even say that God himself has died our death as Son. But at the same time God remains the Father who awakens his Son from the dead. Altizer fears here a return of the Father in the Son, just as Willi Marxsen is opposed to a resurrection which is a return of the earthly life. But first of all let it be said once again that the Father or the Creator does not alienate us from ourselves, that the Father is not merciful because he had first to receive satisfaction and thus in essence would remain the same who absorbs us. Rather the Father remains the initiative of love, which revealed itself in Jesus' life and in his death. Consequently, the Father bestows himself through the glorified Son—or rather, through the Son affirmed in his service and self-abandonment—in a new way—in the Spirit. And thus Jesus too is powerfully present: "the Lord is the Spirit." When Altizer merely salvages "the Great Humanity Divine" he is not, in spite of the title of his book, a complete atheist. If he were, then he would also have had to omit the adjective "divine." He could rather be called pantheist. And perhaps his message remains open along these lines for the faith in the Spirit which comes over us and dwells in us and leads us to the full truth.

In our christological study we have limited ourself solely to christology and have not discussed the Spirit. Indeed, in all our theology to date we have discussed it rather little. We have, in fact, not yet got as far as the Spirit, and consider it an advantage not to have complicated the theology of the *unio hypostatica* by reflections on the Spirit. But it is precisely the modern crisis in our understanding of God, precisely the theology of the death of God, which refers us to the Spirit and Life-Giver.

There is a growing tendency among modern Christians to turn away from the God of religion, who concentrates everything in himself and is all-absorbing. This is a healthy tendency, for God himself is different and has shown himself abundantly different in Jesus Christ. Paraphrasing St. Paul, we could say that God lets peoples go slowly along the paths of religion and permits partial glimpses of himself—for he is close to us. He has also allowed his chosen people slowly and laboriously to break away from religion— here we are using this word in the sense of Altizer, Robinson, Bonhoeffer, Barth. Even the people of God, who are the Church of Jesus Christ, have had to tread that slow and laborious path. Today especially they are called to purify themselves from all religion which alienates them from man on earth, whether this religion be directed towards the Father or towards the glorified *kyrios Pantocrator*. Today more than ever we are told, "Men of Galilee, why do you stand looking into heaven?" We are in the era of the Holy Spirit, and this may prove especially relevant today: in this respect the insight of a Joachim of Fiore is correct.

This is not to say that a completely different salvific economy has dawned, but that what God has bestowed in his Christ is offered in a new actuality. The Father and the Son have not disappeared, on the contrary they are fully present, but precisely in the Spirit—and not primarily in the Spirit of the speaking in tongues, but in the peaceful Spirit who interprets modern history in prophecy, in wisdom and knowledge, who gives discernment and rejects false spirits, who awakens to guidance, help, and healing. One can say the God and Christ are present in the modest, the calm Spirit, the everyday Spirit.

The Spirit has no face but is reference. The Roman liturgy invokes the Spirit, but scarcely ever prays to the Spirit. Perhaps this modest presence of the good Guest of souls—but of whom Paul says that precisely our bodies are his temple—can be our guide in finding God in things and men, and not primarily behind or above them. God remains the transcendent one, precisely through his overwhelming immanence. He is mystery, but precisely through the power with whom he works *in us:* thus he surpasses anything we can evoke, expect, or apprehend. Then we do not have God behind our back as the dead God of religion, but his Spirit is a force at our back, a light in order for us to look, not primarily to heaven but to earth. At the same time, however, God is *"le Dieu d'en-avant,"* for the Spirit is pledge of future, indeed of ultimate future. Much is dark in our time, but it is this hope and this faith we wished to express here.

I believe in God to whom we in Jesus' Spirit may say "Abba, Father," the creative source and future.

And in Jesus, God's Servant and well-beloved Son.

Who came to us completely from God and in whom God's whole fullness dwells bodily.

Who worked for our healing, who transcended human limitations and spoke words of eternal life.

Who for that reason was rejected but suffered for the sake of our liberation and died on the cross.

Who was resurrected by God to live in us and to be the center of the future of all creation.

I believe in the Spirit of God and of Jesus, who speaks through prophets and leads us to the full truth.

I confess God's kingdom now and in eternity, and the Church which may expect and serve this kingdom.

I confess the liberation from sins and the power to love.

And the new creation in which justice dwells and God will be all in all.

Index

189